Fieldsports, Foraging and Terrible Ordeals

by

Robin Bennett

Illustrations *by* Jude Bennett

Fieldsports, Foraging and Terrible Ordeals
(Monster Books Ltd).

Originally published in Great Britain by
Monster Books, The Old Smithy,
Henley-on-Thames, Oxon. RG9 2AR.
Published in November 2023.

Hardback ISBN 9798865541639
Paperback ISBN 9798865537038

A catalogue record of this book is available
from the British Library.

Typesetting/layout
medievalbookshop.co.uk

January
IN WHICH A GOOSE IS COOKED

When I was about seven years old, my father woke one morning and told us, in all seriousness, that not another day could go by without him tasting the sweet flesh of a goose.

He packed me, our cairn terrier, Judy, and his shotgun into our rusting Morris Marina and strapped a canoe onto the roof rack. Then he set off for the river.

I had my doubts even at the early stages of this enterprise: it was January and freezing cold. On top of this, my father had never expressed a craving for goose before, so I felt pretty sure it would soon pass if the call was left unanswered. However, at seven years old, you just kind of go along with things – especially if your father is anything like mine.

We arrived at a bleak stretch of the Thames somewhere near Reading and prepared everything whilst watching the flock of Canada geese lounging about on an island in the middle of the river. Then we got in the canoe: me at the front with the dog; my father at the back, armed to the teeth.

The few walkers who were braving the weather that morning jumped in the air and looked about in alarm as the first shot rang out. Only the goose my father had picked for his dinner seemed unperturbed, as the pellets simply bounced off the thick mattress of breast feathers from twenty yards away.

Undeterred and completely unaware of the sharp looks he was getting from the bank, my father reloaded and paddled closer.

When the second shot rang out, taking the unfortunate goose's head off, people really stopped to stare.

Several things happened rather quickly after that:

My father (still armed) jumped out of the canoe, retrieved a limply flapping goose and threw it on my lap; he then jumped back in, sliding the shotgun down the side of the canoe; whereupon the shotgun's second barrel went off, with a sort of muffled bang; *and we started to sink*. My father panicked: he threw me onto the bank of the island, along with the dog; paddled as fast as he could across the river in a leaking boat; jumped out of the canoe with the shotgun in one hand, the dead goose in the other; and scampered towards the car.

Then he drove off.

It had been an eventful few minutes, but the next part of the morning went very slowly indeed as I stood on that cold island with the dog and wondered what would happen next.

Eventually a put-upon-looking lockkeeper appeared on the opposite bank, got into a small motor launch and made his way across to where I stood. He picked me up, muttering something about a phone call, and took me back to shore to meet my father – who'd had time to go home, wash the blood off and hide the goose.

Two weeks later, we would be sitting in front of the TV with trays on our laps watching Tom Baker being Doctor Who and stuffing our faces with goose. The whole operation was pronounced a great success.

February

PIGEON,
SUNROOF SHOOTING
AND THE SHEER JOY OF PUFF PASTRY

Genteel poverty makes me think of crumbling vicarages, labradors for central heating and a sort of dignified respectability. You can hold your nerve as long as the Aga doesn't pack in. The reality – for us – was more boring: it meant eating a lot of cheese sandwiches with just the merest scraping of butter, and no central heating, all in a crap modern house.

It was very far from terrible, but it wasn't exactly a ball, either.

The estate we lived on in one of the less salubrious parts of Reading had only just been thrown up and it already looked like it wasn't going to see it through to the 1990s.

Whilst everyone we knew went about the place in skinny Adidas t-shirts and those trainers with go-faster stripes, we had to walk into town via one or two council estates wearing identical blue corduroys and Arran sweaters with bobbles that were thick enough to stop a bullet. Posh but poor is not a good look.

On a fairly major level, shooting geese wasn't so much a sport as a practical necessity: if we wanted to eat decent meat on a regular basis, then poaching it would be.

My father came home one day just before Christmas with something long and thin under his arm. I'd had enough experience of communal Christmas presents not to get my hopes up:

to date we'd had a yoghurt maker, a haircutting set and a tent that had leaked – slowly at first, then it felt like you were being rained on indoors. I know this because my father decided to take us up to the Ridgeway in Berkshire to do a spot of illegal camping whilst my mother was giving birth to my sister. It was bitterly cold – because the Ridgeway nearly always is – and because it was February. Then we had a storm with the sort of freezing wind and rain that is designed to get under and into any tent. Ours was no exception. The fact we only lived a few miles away and could have easily got back in the car and gone home to sleep in a dry bed was neither here nor there: Scott had stuck it out, and so would we.

Anyway, the slim package turned out to be an even slimmer gun – a .410 with a single barrel that would fold in half, so you could stuff it down your trousers. Essentially what was consider- ed a child's gun was also perfect for spiriting around the English countryside in a clandestine fashion. It was a gun for getting up to no good. And it coincided with us also getting a car with a sunroof. For most families, this would have been seen as an op- portunity to enjoy the light and wind on your face on pleasant days. For our family it meant we had a turret.

Pretty quickly, the male contingent of the family came up with a very workable strategy for shooting pigeons without permission. This necessitated taking the dog for a long walk, somewhere nice but, at the same time, hiding the little .410 in the car somewhere, out of sight of other motorists, people on horses and the police, but within easy reach. Travel rugs were handy. Someone young and who looked morally untarnished (me) carried the ammunition.

Once the dog had been walked, and the light was fading, we would take the long way home. Just before dusk was an ideal time because the pigeons were roosting and there were less people about. This was about 1975, so before joggers and middle-aged men on mountain bikes existed.

The best sort of trees were usually great big ones, close to the lane, covered in ivy. These are pigeon trees and we got good at spotting them and pointing them out to my father in the way that normal seven-year-old children point at cows and ice cream vans from car windows.

6

My father would slow to a stop, and we'd scan branches and the ivy for signs of movement.

'THERE!' (we always used stage whispers).

Being entirely manual, the sunroof would be cranked open by the child in the front, inch by grating inch. At this point we'd be watching the pigeon whilst holding our collective breath – they seem to have a knack for spotting folk doing anything other than going about their Human Business, ignoring Pigeon Kind.

Tension in the car would be steadily mounting if the pigeon stayed put and I have to admit, at our age and situation in life, it really didn't get any more exciting than this.

As Boy Number One opened the hatch, Boy Number Two would be sliding our gun out and making an important decision: 3-inch cartridges had a better kill potential but made more noise. If we could get away with it, two and a half inches would do or even the much quieter 2-inch cartridges. Also, if the pigeon was too close, you didn't want to 'pillowcase' it: the less full of spent ammunition when it eventually went in the oven, the better.

My father would be watching us with half an eye but mainly keeping a careful lookout on the road for responsible adults. Time was very much of the essence. As was ranking: shots were taken on a strict rotation system, unless a substantially better shot could be taken by whoever was in the front seat. Line of sight was the trump card no-one wanted to play but any ruling favoured who was more likely to get a kill.

We took it as the norm for siblings across the land to frequently have hissy, who's-going-to-shoot-the-pigeon-illegally-from-the-car arguments.

Once the roof was fully open and an assassin picked, the casual observer would have been pushed, unless they were very close, to spot the long, slim barrel telescoping out of the car, like an antenna, as my brother or I loaded it in the same well-practiced movement.

One concrete rule was no loading before the barrel was pointing outside and another was no taking the safety catch off until a second or so before you were ready to squeeze the trigger.

The other logistical problem in the number of logistical problems that were mounting up was Judy, our Cairn terrier, who would by now be beginning to suspect something wonderful was going on. Judy looked like one of those toy dogs you get in shops that bark and do backflips. In reality, she was a psychopath – the member of the family keenest on killing but also the biggest liability.

After a few incidents when she spotted the gun, picked up on the vibe in a doggie way and then ruined a kill by clambering over seats, barking and spreading mud about, we took measures. So, the walk was essential to make sure that before we went looking for pigeons, she was knackered and – preferably – lying under the heater in the footwell of the car, not in the boot, where she could see what was going on.

At this point the pigeon could always fly off and we'd be back to square one or someone would come around the corner and we'd have to pull away as the gun was unloaded and hidden. Another outcome would have been an only slightly dead pigeon that needed the dog and 2 × boys to scramble out of the car and hopefully retrieve – and a lot of explaining to do if there were witnesses. A good kill was a clean kill, an even better one was the bird falling through the open sunroof and us driving off, cackling like Mexican bandits.

The deal at home was:

$$6 \geq p = \pi$$

After the first pie, this became a huge incentive for us all. Up until then, pastry for me had always been a tasteless slab – rock-hard on one side with the consistency of wallpaper paste on the other. But the late '70s was all about experimentation: cheese and wine parties (with pineapple chunks!), Wall's Viennetta and Spandex. In the spirit of progress, my mother used puff pastry and we were hooked. The juices from the pigeon soaked into the pastry, which would already be melting in your mouth as you

hit the rich, chewy breast. Puff was the form a caring and generous Universe had always intended for pastry – the other sort
had merely been an evolutionary process, consigned to a more
basic and brutal past. Fluffy mash, fried carrot slices (never
fucking *batons*), and cold milk to wash it down.

The distinct possibility of coming across spent ammunition
just made it all the more exotic – like a sort of macabre figgy
pudding.

We went through Oxfordshire's pigeon population like it was
a zombie apocalypse and all the shops were shut.

March

RABBITS AND BOARDING SCHOOL CUISINE

A nd things were slowly developing on the home front. Post army, my father's career in the drinks industry had begun to get traction and he was able to fund sending us to a small boarding school in Berkshire.

Think Ron Weasley in patched bellbottoms and that was pretty much me at prep school.

But I didn't give a monkey's butt what I looked like: from the first minute I walked through the mock-Tudor doors of the Oratory Prep School, I decided that this was the place for me. St Joseph's dormitory, of about fifteen other seven-to-eight-year-olds in bunk beds with horsehair mattresses and sheets like sailcloth, still reminds me of that scene in *Oliver* (well, the musical movie version from the 1960s) when Oliver is brought back to Fagin's lair by the Artful Dodger. The school worked for us because the first rule of any good child's narrative is Get Rid of the Parents.

I went back a couple of years ago with my wife – not just to snoop about but because we were prospective fee-payers: legitimately nosey.

Not much appeared to have changed at all and I was really chuffed about that because they were five happy years, by and large. These days, the grounds look more pristine and the pitches better-drained. I do remember an English jungle of giant rhubarb and parsley, next to some broken greenhouses that had both gone but the corridors had kept that warm wood and wax smell, and a quick visit to the bogs confirmed that Tusk is still a bender.

Back in 1977 and being my father's son, one of the first things I did, on arrival at the school, was set rabbit snares in the scrub between the 1st team rugby pitch and Out-of-Bounds.

Once I'd caught one, I then had the problem of what to do with it. I briefly considered presenting my kill to one of the school cooks in the hope she would skin, prepare and serve it on a platter, exclusively to me, instead of Sunday night fish fingers and generic-branded baked beans. But I suspected that awkward questions would be asked, so I gave the rabbit to the school dog, which was pretty bloody generous given as the week before he'd stolen an almost full *sherbet dip dab* from my bare hands.

It got me thinking though, and when I came back from an exeat weekend at home, I had a lighter I'd pinched from my dad's cigar box and a very sharp knife.

I just needed to find a place to skin and barbecue the rabbits now.

This was not too hard: almost half the school grounds were covered in trees. The main wood, leading off down the hill that eventually turned into suburban Reading, looked like forestry commission pine: closely planted with sloping branches that almost touched the ground. I rejected this as being far too scary: even now, I get twitchy when it comes to being anywhere with less ambient light than your average supermarket or dental surgery. I opted, instead, for much friendlier beech woods near where I'd caught my first rabbit and set about building a camp in a hollow.

I'd made friends with a boy in my year, Jace, and he agreed (reluctantly, and more out of politeness) to help me build my camp. Jace was a gentle boy, with a nice temperament and a good sense of humour, but definitely not the outdoors type. I've made friends with him on social media in the last few years and I'd say he was more the *indoors with colour-matched scatter cushions and Italian boyfriend in micro shorts lounging on a white leather sofa* type these days.

I'm not sure he knew that the purpose of the camp was for roasting game, but he went along with the planning and building with enough enthusiasm that soon – by stripping some pine trees in the Brothers Grimm sector of the woods and making a basic a frame between two trees – we had made something primitive but pretty much waterproof.

Then we set about making a fire and a sort of poor man's version of an Argentinian barbecue, Gaucho Style, where the newly-skinned and paunched rabbit was skewered on a stick and leant over the embers.

Quite frankly the results were not exactly what I promised Jace. Rabbit – especially older rabbit – tastes dry and there's something almost metallic about the meat when roasted on a makeshift spit. It was better than the school food in our teetering-on-the-edge-of-bankruptcy boarding school in the 1970's but not by much. Jace made a brave effort – pulling off a leg, Viking stylee – then let himself down by barely managing a queasy nibble. He left the rest to me, which I finished, but mainly out of bravado.

Anyway, even then, I wasn't sure setting traps was my cup of tea.

The whole thing came to an end after I broke my arm and several ribs climbing a tree nearby and the camp was discovered and dismantled.

I've since learned that rabbit needs to be handled carefully. I don't like game that's been left to hang until it's been forgotten about, except by flies. Or until it ends up looking like an extra in a low budget horror movie, in a gibbet. I had an epiphany one evening after years of only eating rabbit when it had been stuffed with bacon or drowned in white sauce. I came back with one after an evening's rough shooting and prepared it immediately – no hanging, just skinned and paunched on arrival. Then I made an oil marinade (no alcohol or vinegar, which will dry the meat) and threw in whatever basic spices I had to hand. The next day, I simply jointed it and put it on the barbecue until the meat started to sizzle. And it was delicious – somewhere between very young chicken and frogs' legs, if you've ever had them and they were fresh.

Now, on my mother's side I was brought up to believe that my great-grandfather was a scoundrel who drank and womanised his way through what little remained of the rest of the family fortune in Trinidad. In the last few years there has been some revisionism, but not enough to obscure the fact that the fortune did disappear and my great-grandfather was forced to flee to Britain.

His choice of the UK was explained by the existence of a cousin who 'owned a chain of restaurants' in London. In reality, 'London' turned out to be Slough and the chain turned out to be one run-down pub in Shaggy Calf Lane that my great-grand-father was supposed to manage, whilst housing his entire family in a single room above the snug bar.

His solution to this reversal of fortune was to die right there on the spot; though whether through grief, rage or sheer bloody mindedness, I really don't know.

It still ranks as the most extreme way of turning down a job I've come across.

I mention this (and I promise to get back to rabbits in a bit) because it's kind of interesting but also by way of comparison with my paternal grandparents who were of a more traditional breed altogether.

The fire was lit at 4pm for tea – not a moment before – almost everything was homegrown: from the lambs, to the orchard full of veg and soft fruits that circled the sort of English garden you only see in costume dramas.

They did have a Teasmade: one concession to modern life that was otherwise steadfast country Edwardian.

For so many years of my life, my paternal grandparents'

home, Woodhayes, was the rural idyll we almost all long for in some way. In spite of the possibility of getting no more than two inches of hot water in a bath if you were lucky, it was the place I looked forward to going to more than anywhere on the planet: for holidays that were a sort of freedom to my brother and me that you couldn't get in the Home Counties in a semi-urban environment; then as a refuge from boarding school on half terms; and, finally, as a focus for the nostalgia of childhood, on middle-age pilgrimages whenever I found myself in the area.

The living room, with its sponge cake for teatime, smelled of old sofa and wood fire. The Aga gave us chilblains more often than not, but still felt like the womb of the house. I loved the thatch and the whitewashed walls, the smell of dust and oil in the barn, and the whole welly boot scraping, wind racking to the point of breath-taking, dried flower arranging, blazing fire, giant tractor tyre, dog-friendly thing. The garden was a minia-ture Eden. It had a year-round supply of things to eat: straw-berries the size of a child's fist, gooseberries that made you wince, windfall Russets and Victoria plums we would split open with the heal of our hand to check for bugs then scoff on the sly.

At Woodhayes I experienced what it is like to have a spiritual home and how that anchor becomes a rock.

On a practical level, I learned about how to keep lambs – the rudiments of ruminants, split logs, dam streams, spin for mack-erel and refine my poaching skills ...

In spite of myxomatosis, the south-facing slopes (that didn't belong to us) had armies of rabbits, almost invisible against the summer-burned tussocks of grass, until they heard you stomp-ing up the hill and fled, their tails bobbing like those plumes atop hussars' hats. *Watership Down* was a big deal at the time, so warrens always felt like military divisions to me.

The tools we had weren't great. My grandfather's .177 air rifle really was a bit of a wreck but the only alternative was a solid lump of low grade steel in the form of a Belgium 12 bore of no particular pedigree that my brother and I could hardly lift, let alone fire.

So, the air rifle it had to be. For some reason, perhaps because the barrel was slightly bent, it tended to shoot like a banana. The challenge, then, was two-fold – well, three, really, I'll come onto that in a bit.

First of all, you had to get far closer to them than you normally would if shooting with a decent shotgun (forty yards) or a .22 rifle (roughly one hundred and twenty yards). To be effective, we were looking at around twelve yards – fifteen absolute max.

This was tricky and gave rise to problem Number Two: rabbits with their comedy large ears that they can swivel about like a party trick. This allows them to hear things just under two miles away (according to bunny experts). As if that isn't unsporting enough, your average rabbit is also the proud owner of around one hundred million scent cells, compared to our own measly five or six million. And they've got those large, doe eyes on the sides of their heads, which not only makes them look cute (and therefore makes you a terrible person for wanting to cook them) but it gives all round, three-hundred-and-sixty-degree vision.

Finally, bunnies are incredible scaredy cats, which isn't surprising, given how many species find them delicious. Once one gets spooked, they all make a run for it and our stupid predator brains then find it very hard to discern which adorable, white-tailed, bottom to pick on.

However, we did figure out a couple of techniques that worked for us roughly thirty percent of the time, which we could live with. Time for some bullet points!

- Don't have the wind at your back (obviously).
- Walk slowly, steadily and try not to make any noise (or my big brother will give you a dead leg, I guarantee it). They'll definitely hear you with those bionic ears of theirs, but we found that the alternative – i.e., irregular, stop-start walking is viewed by rabbits as Suspicious Walking [which] = *stop nibbling bits of grass and go into Antenna Ear Mode.* Breaking sticks, stubbing your feet on rocks, burping = *run like fucking hell.*
- If you can see the rabbit, they can **definitely** see you.

However, we found that if we picked the one facing away from us or was directly head on, for some reason they didn't seem to mind or notice you getting closer – just as long as you didn't veer even a few centimetres left or right.

This last point is linked to the third challenge in the process. Not only was it a good idea, from a hunting point of view, to remain invisible for as much of the process as possible, but it was also quite important for legal reasons: We were trespassing, poaching and we probably shouldn't have been armed at all at our age.

My grandparents' small wood helped, as we could lurk within its shadowy fringes, but the ground was quite sticky – in that it was covered in sticks (not jam).

So, we learned to walk just beyond the overhanging branches. Still in dappled light, but with springy, soft and silent grass underfoot.

Before any of this could start, Charles and I had to get rid of the dog. Judy really couldn't be trusted in any rough shooting scenario invented: she was noisy, almost absurdly badly-behaved and wedded to violence. As far as she was concerned, if anything was going to die, it would be by her paw alone and in the most bloodthirsty, chaotic and harrowing way imaginable. The irony being her presence absolutely guaranteed that no rabbits would ever be shot. If dogs as crap as Judy went hunting on a regular basis, Planet Earth would now be run by rabbits and pheasants.

If we left her in the house, my grandmother – who was a gentle soul and didn't approve of killing rabbits (or locking bad dogs up) – would let her out and she would be racing over to wherever we were creeping about as fast as her stumpy, terrier legs could carry her. I'd seen her burst out of the wood and throw herself into our firing line, almost as if she was trying to save the rabbits, as opposed to ripping them to shreds with her teeth.

All dogs, deep down, think they're still Timber Wolves, even if they're only one foot tall and frankly a bit dim. Bursting in on Judy whilst she was having a late afternoon nap and shouting 'Where is it?' in a panicky voice would have her fully awake and bashing her head against the door in under four seconds. Asking her where something was could only mean one thing, to her way of thinking: the barn was under attack. Quite why she was convinced my grandparents' barn was in a permanent state of mortal danger, I've really no idea, but one of us would have the door of the barn open whilst the other would open the back door and Judy would race across the courtyard, barking ferociously, straight into the barn. And the door would slam shut behind her.

A quick tour of the barn, the discovery it wasn't full of cats eating filet mignon and the fact we hadn't followed her could only mean one thing ... she'd been duped again.

Judy's howls of anguish would follow our guilty ears as we picked up the air rifle, crossed the orchard, climbed over the fence and into the field where our grandparents kept their sheep, and down to the spinney.

Half an hour later in the stillness of the approaching dusk, we would be closing in on our quarry.

With any luck.

The last twenty yards would be the most intense, as you committed to one rabbit, kept the pace slow but regular and watched fixedly for signs it was spooked and might bolt. To get me to concentrate to that degree on anything else when I was that age would have required hypnosis and a head clamp. Reading, sport, even television would never get close to the same level of focus where my breathing, movement, mind and vision had tunnelled into one point of focus.

Deciding when to shoulder the rifle and take a shot was key and had to be smooth and quick. But never too quick. The rabbit would always tense as the rifle came up, its shoulders bunching as it saw a movement and was thinking about running. But we'd learned not to hurry: even at that point, you usually had about three seconds to steady your aim, think about your breathing and squeeze the trigger.

As I say, only about thirty percent of the time did we manage to get close enough to have a realistic chance and I'd say only about another third of the time we were able, did the rabbit stay put long enough to fire and the shot was accurate enough to kill or stop it. Looking back, we had very few injured escapees, I think because we were so close, the fifteen-yard rule was sound from a humanitarian point of view. This was also thanks to my brother, whose natural restraint acted as a brake to my enthusiasm to come home every night with a kill.

But those rare-ish times, when you got your supper and you walked home with it, felt burnished, like the copper sun that slipped behind the gorse-tufted hills. In those moments, our life belonged to us, with no rules, nor adults ... or even small, scruffy dogs to intrude.

April

IN WHICH WE GO MUSHROOMING,
BUT FIND A POTHOLE INSTEAD
AND THERE IS UNFORTUNATE INCIDENT
WITH A LUMP HAMMER
THAT WE ALL REGRET, IN HINDSIGHT

One of the best things about Dorset was the bungalow my grandparents purchased in West Bay and where we would sometimes stay, instead of inland, in their thatched cottage. As investments went, I don't think it was astute: flat-roofed and squat, it looked alarmingly flimsy for something so close to the actual sea. It also smelled of seaweed and somehow managed to be freezing cold even in the height of August.

That said, we loved it.

For us, West Bay represented a level of freedom you can usually only read about or see in old films – most parents talk tough when it comes to avoiding mollycoddling but a sizeable majority baulk when it comes to letting ten-year-old kids roam about near lots of choppy water.

Not us, predictably enough. As soon as we woke up, we were allowed to leave the bungalow and Get Up To Stuff. We developed a routine: the first order of the day was chucking stones into the grey waves on the beach right opposite, as we gradually edged down the front to the small harbour where flatter water meant we could skim stones until something more interesting came along. This was usually in the form of the West Bay fishing fleet arriving back, filled with crabs who would wave their claws at us through the rope bars of their cages as they passed. And we would wave back jauntily. Then we'd follow them in, because mooching around the market, there was always the possibility of finding a stray fish part on the ground and putting it in your brother's hood when he wasn't looking.

Although it was probably only 8am, the amusement arcade would almost certainly be open by now – a bit like those pubs that seem to keep irregular hours to cater for professional alcoholics. This had been our goal all along. And we were really only interested in three games: Space Invaders came third, Formula One a close second – the racing seat was disconcertingly damp and smelled curiously sweet but in an unwholesome way – like piles of rotting apples. Hands down best of all, was an armoured vehicle game that used actual models of tanks across a papier-mâché landscape – with speakers to relay pre-recorded sound effects such as the clanking of metal tracks across fields, turrets grinding into position, explosions and flames. I'm tempted to say it would probably be a bit crap now – you know, by modern standards and all. But I bet it wouldn't be – I reckon it would still be brilliant.

If it rained for more than two days in a row by the sea, we'd start to roam inland. I've always liked coastal towns with beaches that are overlooked by cows and bordered by paths that lead up cliffs and into green fields as opposed to broad expanses of sand that are essentially deserts. The nearby countryside served as a means to escape the seaside brashness that can get to you after a bit, and tramping about in the English drizzle, in a meadow is somehow nicer than being on a wet pier or cloggy by the beach.

It was there we learned that puffballs aren't just for stamping on. Taken home and fried in butter they weren't exactly what you'd call delicious, but they have a satisfyingly squidgy texture. Even better – especially since they were available when we came down for the Easter holidays – were Jelly Ears. I think these are considered a 'Super Food' now – a bit like chard but less horrible and not as wanky as quinoa. Anyway, I'm told they're amazingly good for colds and infections but the main attraction – when you're young – is they look and feel just like real ears.

We'd gather them up and get our mum to put them in soup or stews that were essential fodder in that freezing cold house by the sea. Then, with the sea flattened by wind and strafed by rain, we'd go out looking for more stuff in the countryside.

And, lo, it was on one of these expeditions we found our cave.

From the outside it didn't look like much at all: ordinary field (grass, hedge, cow or two), a moderately undulating terrain but nothing you'd associate with proper speleology, per se. And a tufted outcrop you'd not really dwell on, unless you were dawdling about, whilst looking for free food in the form of edible fungi.

But there, at the foot of the outcrop there was a fissure in the compacted earth. Like an invitation. A closer look gave rise to the exciting discovery that the rent widened into a tunnel proper. Cool air blew on our faces from within, carrying the scent of damp earth, space and the very achievable prospect of something even more fun than picking mushrooms.

We were delighted. England has never been a very 'cavey' place in my experience and those ones we have are usually fenced off or part of an expensive day out, where you have to be patient and queue up.

My father, brother and I squeezed through and peered about as best we could. My dad started lighting matches, which either blew out immediately or lit up an area about the volume of your average bucket before burning his fingers and going out.

There was nothing for it, we'd have to get tooled up and come back.

I think there must have been a delay in us finding the time to return. This may have been for wholly innocent reasons, such as family outings or going to the shops or was down to the fact my father couldn't tell my mother what we were planning. So, an opportune moment needed to be found when she had gone out with my baby sister and wouldn't query why we were gathering torches, ropes and other highly suspicious bits of kit by the back door to our temporary seaside accommodation. As it was, most of our equipment was filched from my grandparents' main house down the road. And this is where I probably over-thought it.

When preparing for an expedition, once you start asking yourself 'what if ...', you'll end up taking flares and a machete on a family picnic. By the time I was ready to go, I was swathed in ropes, waddling about in gigantic walking boots and seriously considering an old motorbike helmet. I must have been persuaded to keep my girth to a minimum, on account of all the squeezing into tight spaces I'd be required to do, but I do remember insisting on jamming a lump hammer in my belt as an afterthought. I was sure would come in useful if we had to excavate ourselves out of trouble.

Looking back, this was a mistake.

Nevertheless, at that stage we were feeling confident as we walked towards the pothole. No-one was about as we took it in turns to slip inside its dank antechamber and we turned our torches on. I remember that I was old enough to know that it was a good idea to keep my hopes to a manageable level, so I was part-resigned to discovering our 'cave' petered out after a few yards with signs of a half-hearted fire, fag buts and old beer cans. We'd already explored a few promising hollows around Lyme Regis that turned out to be cubby holes for drinking beer and/or pooing.

But the pothole not only continued a good distance, it fanned out and felt like a proper cavern – minus paintings and stalag-mites ... but still. This was absolutely brilliant, but not half as cool as when we got to the end and discovered a deep shaft.

In silence we pointed out torches down the chimney. There was a drop of about forty feet and the diameter was probably three feet. Most enticing was the fact the bottom looked dry, almost sandy and, as our beams played about, we could see there was a sort of archway to the left, that led off somewhere even more interesting.

Short of finding a pirate skeleton lying beside a casket and a sword, this was about as good as it got.

I can't remember why, but it was decided that my father would climb down first, chimney sweep-style, followed by me. Perhaps my brother, the more prudent, was posted at the top in case anything went wrong. I can't remember, but what definitely did happen is my dad went first and, after a decent-ish interval, I followed.

I guess I must have been about halfway down when the hammer fell out of my belt.

I guess my father must have been two thirds down, so – not to seem like I'm making light of it – he did overreact a little bit when then falling hammer hit him on the head with a comedy DOINK! and he fell all the way (a few feet – seven, max) to the bottom.

... the trick with my father's rages was to keep out of his way until he cooled off. However, the problem with arms when you're seven is they're a bit spindly and crap. There was no way I could climb back up, but there was no way I was going down until he cooled off.

The weird, subterranean Mexican standoff carried on with him swearing and shouting at me to come down, until I think he realised it was getting in the way of the adventure, so slowly, getting assurances I wasn't going to come to terrible physical harm, I descended.

In the end, our adventure pretty much stopped there. The tunnel continued but not by much and my dad was a bit quiet. He may have had a headache.

He climbed back up and I had a minute or so trying not to panic on my own until a rope came down and it was my turn to be dragged back into the ante chamber. As we walked back to the car, my brother gave me a *what were you thinking* look but nothing more was said about the hammer. It's probably still lying down there with my father's DNA on it, which is a macabre thought.

Finding a hole in the ground that turned out to be a real pot-hole is a childhood standout memory. That said, I've never really got into caving since. On the other hand, foraging for free food, learned young, doesn't easily leave you and we were only just getting started.

May

COCKLES & CANOES.
WHY TRYING TO FEED YOURSELF
FROM ROCKPOOLS IS BETTER THAN
WASTING YOUR TIME ON DIY.
ENGLISH BEACHES V. FRENCH BEACHES

Some years ago, shortly after I'd grown up and become a proper adult, we bought a house in France at a time when something modest but characterful cost the price of a car in the UK. These days, we don't get to go back as often as we would like but at the start of last autumn, I nipped across for some early season shooting to find our perfectly flat wooden flooring in France had gone rogue. It now undulated like waves in a small harbour.

After previous incidents, that I would call 'learning experiences', but my French wife talks about as national catastrophes on a par with the Eiffel Tower disappearing into a sinkhole, I solemnly gave my word I would never touch another power tool as long as we both drew breath.

Nevertheless, as soon as H. had gone to the shops, I binned any thoughts of going out with the dog to try and shoot one of the four pheasants that were skulking somewhere in the vast expanse of maize outside our back door, changed my trousers and went to the barn instead ... with a great sense of optimism. I was on the hunt for a jigsaw I bought when I built a kitchen (badly) in our Clapham flat in about 1997.

The problem was simple: the floor had expanded in the heat and was too 'long'.

I would make it shorter.

It was a win-win – we'd be back to non-corrugated flooring, and everyone would be so impressed I could revert to my old ways of taking a lump hammer and gaffer tape to any DIY problem around the house.

Turns out jigsaws have a shelf life. Since I had last used ours it had got used to its retirement. Seconds after I turned it on, flames with sparks started coming out of the plastic casing as I flayed about with it in my hand. Briefly, I looked like Zeus.

Coming to my senses, I turned it off at the wall and spent the next five minutes getting my breathing and pulse back to normal before deciding that it was only a minor blip and I would press on.

Old school, I thought when I noticed the plane; *back to basics*. From woodwork lessons at school, I remembered the calming effect planing wood has on a person and, sure enough, within five minutes I was even thinking of a career change: I would turn my back on Mammon, lead a simple and good life. I would *carpent* (= repent + woodwork).

Time passed and my soul healed.

When I finally blew off all the shavings, I saw that my work had done the trick: the bit of flooring in my hand was noticeably thinner. Hang on, it was much thinner.

The cold dark shadow of foreboding fell across the worktable, and I walked slowly back to the house with a rising sense of dread.

I think now is the time to tell you about our underlay.

Underlay, in my experience, is usually a neutral colour: rus-set, Sherwood green or taupe. For some reason, ours is made of the sort of super shiny material cute female aliens on '70s epi-sodes of *Star Trek* always wear. Captain Kirk was always a sucker for gold lamé.

The underlay now shone through the floor with the intensity of the sun. It was as if I had just chiselled away the planking to discover a hidden world – a happier place of light and colour below our feet.

Perhaps that's how I would sell it to H.?

Bollocks, I thought, reality flooding in, *that won't even work on the children. Nothing for it, I will have to cover my tracks.*

Mastek will be my friend.

26

It's things like this that convince me my family genetics didn't get much past the hunter-gatherer period. Certainly not as far as the settle down and build things stage of human development.

Even as far back as the mid-70s, DIY – glue, in particular – was at top of our shopping list. Particularly one cold April morning as we looked at the pieces of our broken canoes strewn across the A303.

A combination of the car picking up speed on a brief stretch of dual carriageway and a nasty cross wind had lifted the canoes enough to snap whatever was keeping them attached to the car and sent them tumbling, very alarmingly, behind us. Luckily, it was into empty road – it was at some ungodly hour of the morning, and no-one was about – otherwise things could have been a lot worse.

I was told it wasn't safe to hang about gawping at the broken canoes, so I walked gingerly back to the car. As half term holidays went, this had definitely had its moments. Firstly, I was hobbling because I was barefoot, the reason for this is I didn't have any shoes. In fact, I hadn't had any for days, not since my only pair were washed away by the tide and the nearest Clarks was deemed too far to paddle to.

Canoeing camping is simply a convenient way of combining just a couple of the many wet and uncomfortable experiences to be had in the British Isles during a Summer Half Term holiday. If you add a lot of wind, because you're by the sea (Poole Harbour, in our case) you end up with an experience where any comfort is hard won and greatly appreciated.

For example, the simple joy of lighting a fire on the beach and finally getting warm after a hard afternoon crossing swirling inhospitable sea the colour of used dishwater beats anything Disneyland Paris has to offer. I really mean that. And the real terror of capsizing trumps the manufactured fear of the rollercoaster, followed by genuine relief when you hit dry land.

The first thing my brother and I would be instructed to do as soon as we got on the beach was to fan out across the beach and look for edible shellfish.

These days we'd be talking rock oysters, scallops and abalone if you're on Guernsey. In 1977, we were decidedly more down-market, so Charles and I would come back with limpets, winkles and the odd mussel, if we were lucky, stuffed into our t-shirts we'd made into temporary bags.

It probably wasn't up to much by today's standards, but I have generally positive memories of the hot seafood soup we made, harvested from rockpools and cooked over a fire in one of those aluminium pots as your jumper finally starts to dry out ... at the front at least.

It's years since I've eaten winkles and whelks in a format other than doused in vinegar with a wooden prong, but my abiding impression is they are surprisingly tasty for something that looks inedible and has the consistency of a tub full of condoms. The same goes for many of the other Things that Cling to Rocks we have eaten as a family, including sea urchins. Who needs friends when you have anemones.

Mussels and oysters are probably the only ones that are really tasty, in their own right, but I guess an important lesson was being learned about appreciation of what you need, rather than what you want – although it probably seemed a little obscure at the time and, anyway, kids don't think like that. Like dogs, the lesson is in the moment: i.e., one moment we were being tipped about on unfriendly sea, frozen and fearing for our lives, the next we weren't: hurrah! Running about barefoot and living off the contents of an English beach is a win after life at sea in something flimsy, built to ply the genteel waters of the Thames.

And I'm probably being unfair about canoeing. True, in the 1970s pretty much half of all kayaks and canoes were made from canvas on a wooden frame which you had to assemble yourself (more glue). If you weren't retired or chronically un-employed and therefore didn't have the required one thousand hours to build it just knocking about in your life, then you bought a fibre glass canoe. It was light, came in a range of garish colours and the fibre glass rubbed off on your bare legs whilst you paddled along in a sort of itchy-pain-filled-purgatory.

But exploring backwaters is fun, being able to handle yourself on water in anything, even one of those giant ducks, is a skill and being trusted to do anything between the ages of about six and twelve feels good.

In between dodging the Jersey ferry and sheltering from the rain with the dog at the bottom of the canoe, we also figured out that it was possible to catch mackerel using cheap metal lures and a combination of spinning and jigging (bouncing the line along the bottom). Mackerel really are the easiest fish to catch in the world and were a great addition to our beach-side feasts with slightly salty/soggy brown bread.

On balance, it was a pretty good holiday. What doesn't kill you makes you stronger or, at least, makes you wary about leaving your Dunlop Greenflashes close to the sea when the tide turns. We didn't just bob about in the water or fish and forage. My dad bought us strawberry Mivvis at Corfe Castle and I saw my first red squirrel on Brownsea Island.

And the canoes, it turned out, were repairable. In fact, they lasted right into my twenties, each glue-daubed streak a testament to one or other accident, or well-at-least-we-can-laugh-about-it-now-without-crying (just about) adventure.

On the subject of beaches, and seeing as this chapter started with a gallic flavour, it might as well finish with one. The French seaside proved to be very different, when we crossed the English Channel a few years later.

My father's job took us to Cognac and coming from striking Britain in 1979, it was like someone had walked into a room at 4.30pm in December and turned the lights on: everything was warmer and brighter.

Like the UK, the seaside was a big draw … but for entirely different reasons.

We went to the beach a lot, and any number of my mum's friends who we'd meet up with would dump bags of towels, picnic baskets and umbrellas next to where I was sitting and take off their clothes. Every last stitch, in some cases.

Up until that point, my appreciation of the female form had

been limited to family members racing from bathroom to bedroom, dawdling through the lingerie section of the Mothercare catalogue when I thought no-one was looking and, one dull Sunday, the discovery of the English master's porn scrapbook hidden in a classroom. This had been typically '70s kitsch: lots of Kate Bush lookalikes standing in fields next to horses, or drippy girls, in soft focus, gaping into mirrors. Their nipples were normally obscured by leaves or the long tresses they were pretending to comb, and each appeared to have a small marsupial between her legs: pants made of hair that left everything to your imagination. The Mothercare catalogue – particularly the maternity bra section – looked positively hardcore by comparison.

But it was now the '80s and depilation had come to France somewhat earlier than the UK. The upshot was you could see *everything*: everything was smooth – like statues I'd seen in museums – and breasts that made the slightest movement excruciatingly exciting.

This was also the first time I had been exposed to the less than perfect form of the female body and, in real life, they seemed to be even more in the nude: childbirth bellies and dark nipples. It was shocking at first, then thrilling.

I looked on from under my blonde fringe at these magnificent women in their thirties and forties: drinking ice-cold rosé, gossiping and scolding children, whilst they slapped cream onto areas that swayed and puckered erotically in the fresh air. What was most appealing was their French insouciance – they were utterly confident in their bodies and all their imperfections: they knew they were sexy, but that wasn't just it – they were also there to talk, to drink, to eat, and bring up their children. They had other stuff going on.

My mother and the other English mums looked on like they'd just stumbled onto the set of a saucy B-movie, where nudes frolicked and quaffed, and children did what they liked. These Home Counties women remained steadfastly on the side lines, clutching the cheese sandwiches they'd made earlier, squeezed into dark M&S one-pieces, their bodies like *boudin blancs*.

Sometimes they remembered to chew.

June
FISHING AND FAMILY LIFE

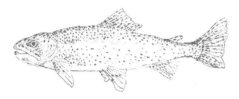

Fast forward eighteen years and my wife and I have a family that still feels like a miracle to me. I've convinced myself that I've left irresponsibly-planned holidays far behind. As a father of three children, I'm careful and accountable. Dull even.

If I didn't have my mind on more pressing things, I might be reflecting on the truth of this … but I'm suspended up to my armpits in icy snow. My feet are pedalling about in what feels suspiciously like a void. I know we're in the French Pyrenees, but it's summertime, so I really hadn't been expecting this amount of ice and snow. We might as well be in the Andes.

I'm not waving my feet about for fun, I'm hoping to find some purchase and trying not to panic. The trickly sound of water below me makes think I've fallen half into a crevice, compacted ice with a frosted covering of snow bridging the gap. How far below I've literally got no idea.

And that's not really the worst bit.

Three small faces look down at the top half of their dad. To be fair, they don't seem overly worried, but they don't know that I've left my mobile phone in the car, the keys to which I felt slip out of my pocket when I partly disappeared thirty seconds ago.

'OK, kids, stay where you are,' I say, but slightly unnecessarily – they're kids, not blithering idiots. The eldest, and therefore most capable, has a recently-broken arm in a caste, so he's not going to be much help.

Pushing myself up risks making the hole much bigger, which will result in me falling through, down into an uncertain future. However, I've really got no option: I've come to a mountain in poor weather conditions, with no means on communication and I've got three children aged eight to twelve in tow, one injured.

So, I take a deep breath and start to haul myself up onto my elbows, then feel the ice bridge creak ominously. I immediately stop doing that and attempt a winning smile instead. This doesn't go down well.

'Daddy, have you hurt yourself?' the youngest asks, starting to look properly worried for the first time.

'Nope,' I say. Fuck it, I think and give an almighty heave. A chunk of ice about the width and depth of a wheelbarrow breaks off but, by the same dumb luck that's followed me about all my life, it's not the important bit. Although my heart is beating like a jackhammer, I find I've managed to claw myself up and across enough ice to be partially back on solid ground.

I look back and see a drop of about nine feet through the newly-formed hole and a stream with lots of uninviting sharp rocks. It wouldn't have killed me, but it would have hurt. And now I must scramble down and delve about in freezing water to find my keys or it's going to be a long walk home.

Twenty minutes later, we're trudging downhill back to the car, wet keys safely in a zipped-up pocket. I'm feeling strangely elated, even though my wife will definitely have something to say when the kids inevitably spill their guts.

Still, the mountains are spectacular: it's sunny, warm and snowy. I get the feeling we should be marching along, swinging our arms and singing. But none of us can carry a tune to save our lives, so I make do with looking about, thinking happy thoughts.

'So, we're not going fly fishing now?' asks Auxiliary Son, Number Two, breaking the mood.

'No,' I reply. 'We're going to MacDonalds.'

I've never had any luck with fly fishing. I've done it in Scotland, France (with an expensive guide, I'm not referring this debacle) and – weirdly – once on the side of Mount Kenya. And I've never caught a thing, never even been close to catching a thing. Which is a shame because I love trout and salmon and I like the idea of fly fishing: everything from the making of flies, to the choosing of a spot, casting, and the open air. I also like rivers.

That said, as I walk back to the car with bruised ribs, I'm still feeling chipper because up until then we'd had a good time throwing snowballs at the start of the walk, sliding about and generally being together – which is what it's all about – in one of my favourite parts of the world.

Hot on the heels of our fly-fishing false dawn, I'm standing in our barn wondering what to do with four pairs of nearly-new waders we'd bought. We'd hauled them up a mountain about an hour's drive from where we live in France, where I was told the fishing was good. I'd even gone online and got a license, then swung by Decathlon to get a couple of basic sets of rods and a box of flies. The waders are still pristine and I thought about taking them back for a refund but the last time I tried taking a croquet set back, the person in the shop asked me where the packaging was.

'It's at home,' I replied. 'But I don't need a refund on that, the packaging was fine – actually it was excellent, it took me several hours to get the croquet set out of it … using power tools and rage. So, I'm keeping it, in case there's a war and I need to build a bomb shelter.'

'Ha ha,' the shop assistant replied with no trace of humour, because the French meet irony with mounting irritation, as a rule. 'But we can't give you a refund for this croquet set unless it is in its original packaging or it is faulty.'

'It was faulty. Well, sort of.'

'How?'

'Well, when I did eventually remove several kilometres of strong tape, multiple layers of reinforced cardboard and enough polystyrene to float Versailles, I found it was tiny. It's a croquet set for dwarves.'

'I can't comment on that,' the assistant replied, looking like they wanted to object to me using the word dwarf. To be honest, I suddenly wasn't sure if that was still allowed as a word for short people.

'Am I going to get a refund?'

'Non.'

A week later lockdown hits and we have another bright idea (about waders, the croquet set is still in our barn, in case elves fancy a game whilst we sleep).

There's a small, chatty river that flows close to our village in its own fold between woodland and water meadow. From the Middles Ages to about the turn of the last century, it formed a small economic hub of watermills. Most are long since abandoned and fallen into attractive ruins with trees supporting the remains of roofs and blackberry bushes tumbling out of windows. This miniature valley is now forgotten and unfrequented and walking alongside it with the dog, you're only likely to meet cows, sheep and wild boar.

During lockdown, Emmanuel Macron decided we weren't to stray more than a kilometre in radius from our houses. Within a few weeks our usual walks had become dull to the point of the dog looking put-upon every time we went out.

Which is how we hit upon the idea of exploring the river with all its lost pockets of civilisation by walking up the actual riverbed itself. Using our pristine waders.

To be honest, I hadn't really banked on how interesting it would turn out to be. For starters, everything looks incredibly different when you're about six foot lower, staring up at overhanging branches and tufts of soft grass: it's being more part of the landscape, because you're actually in it. As for practicalities, the river is only a couple of feet deep in places, flowing over round river stones the colour of dark chocolate or melted toffee. In other places it forms deep pools you need to take slowly, water lapping to the top on the waders. The dog figured out he could keep up by paddling or following via the bank at the deep bits. And that kept him happy as we went places he'd never been, deep into the deserted countryside.

It felt like a new world – in a way, everything did at that time.

From this change in perspective, we noticed holes in the clay sides of the bank: large ones for water rats and smaller ones I suspected were crayfish.

Like the UK, French waterways have been taken over by the larger American crayfish and it's almost considered your civic duty to keep their populations under control, lest they drive the European crayfish to full extinction. That's one plus point, the other two are crayfish are technically easy to catch/cook and delicious.

I'd used streaky bacon and string to catch them in the Thames, so we went for the next best thing – local dried ham. Then I got told off for wasting good food by Mrs B, so we moved to the assorted pheasant, partridge and chicken wings I freeze during the season and feed to the dog. The idea here was once we'd used them for catching our crayfish, I could then put back on the dog's menu, only partly nibbled, but with interesting fishy undertones.

Frankly, the best and most fun way to eat crayfish is on the spot, so it's a good idea to bring along something to boil them in ... and matches. It also means that when you take the edible tails off, you can throw the rest in the river for the pike, in the hope that they will leave the tender and cherished parts of our anatomies alone as we raided upriver.

However, gallic crayfish turn out to be more underhand and cunning than British ones, which is hardly surprising, given their similar propensity in other areas. After discovering the smaller holes were inhabited with a sort of shiny, semi-aquatic black beetle and the larger ones disgruntled *ragondin* (water rats), we shifted our attention to making trout traps in the shallow parts of the river. This is done by piling up stones in a tight horseshoe at a bend in the river, the idea being the trout, swimming downriver, will find itself caught in this natural pool, with its bottleneck entrance. After a couple of fruitless trips to return to the trap to find it empty, we spotted the obvious flaw: namely, it relies on you being there, ready to catch the fish almost immediately because any fish with an ounce of intelligence will quite quickly figure out it just needs to swim back the way it came to escape.

I've since found out you can make it harder for the captured fish by creating elaborate stone defences with waterfalls and oubliettes etc. or maybe they all essentially rely on the fish being lazy and staying put.

Either way it was fruitless but fun, which pretty much sums up fishing as an experience for me.

Eventually, after several outings, we had sploshed all the way to the reedy source of the Lees. Mapping as we went, we pushed up banks to explore the old mills and their crumbling out houses, crawled under lips of clay, tree roots hanging down like mud-caked fingers, scrambled over fallen oaks, beech trees and birch, then lit fires upon which we cooked sausages I'd brought along, in case we finished up empty-handed.

Much is made of childhood memory and so I won't dwell but perhaps we're too coy about the nostalgia of parenthood. Having children still feels like winning the lottery for us and I love the fact they enjoy the countryside the way we do.

Sadly, it seems that far too quickly our children's childhood fades to grey in our recollections – a bit like the countryside at the end of a flawless day, as you walk home through long grass beside flowing waters.

July

THE QUEEN'S STAG

I'm in the Grampians in Scotland, it's late July but it's bloody freezing. The outside air temperature is made a lot worse by the fact I am currently crawling through a small, bitterly cold stream. I am staying as low as I can because the gully the stream is in isn't very deep and there's a group of deer, about two hundred yards away, that we've been creeping up on unsuccessfully all day.

Whoever imagines stalking deer to be glamorous hasn't been stalking deer.

Today we have covered about fifteen kilometres across boggy heather, gritting our teeth, wordlessly jumping from tussock to tussock as we remain downwind and below the contours of the hills that keep us under the radar of the group of stags we spotted with the long telescope earlier that morning.

Victor, has come along. He's eleven and he shot his first grouse yesterday, but I think I'm prouder of the fact that he's covered the tricky terrain today without one word of complaint.

By the time we reach the end of the gully and sneak our heads over a small circle of heather, we're praying the deer haven't already moved off – as they've done a couple of times already. Otherwise, you have to repeat the process of going down into the valley and looking for a way up with cover, which would mean another hour or so hard walking, then more crawling about.

But they are still there, about one hundred and eighty yards away. The ghillie, a young chap from Cumbria, ducks down and we put our heads together. He whispers that it's risky, we're right on the march (border) with Balmoral but there's an old stag who needs culling, to the right of the group. He's a distant shot and sitting down, so we'll have to wait until he gets up, but he's the best we'll get as it's near the end of the day.

It's a long wait and the rifle in my shoulder is shaking because it really is ridiculously cold for late summer. I am also beginning to cramp up.

When the stag eventually stands, all the physical effort and concentration of the day focuses in on the moment I get him in my sights and squeeze the trigger. A stag's heart is about the size of a largish grapefruit. Ideally, I need to hit an area about twenty centimetres in diameter where his front leg joins his torso. At one hundred and eighty yards, cold and tired, it's not a comfortable shot, made harder by the fact that I need to take it quickly as my target's body language tells me he's about to move off at a canter. But the truth is, there is always a risk when you pull the trigger, always a chance you'll just injure an animal. They have to be culled, but a clean kill is really the only humane result.

'It's a kill shot,' the ghillie confirms after I've fired. Nevertheless, the stag has bolted.

'He'll not go more than a few yards, but that's bad,' the ghillie looks worried; 'he's on Balmoral land. How do you feel about poaching?'

'Completely fine,' I say, and I realise, right then, that however far we move away from our roots, or think we do, we don't.

We've left Victor a few hundred yards behind us. The ghillie throws me the keys to the Land Rover. 'Take it round to Loch Muick and as far up into the treeline as you can go without getting bogged down!' he shouts over his shoulder, trying to run and unpack a harness at the same time. 'I'll drag him down the hill and we'll load him up as quickly as possible.' I run the quarter of a mile to the Landy. As I drove around to the spot, I can see a grouse-shooting party coming off the hill on Balmoral land. 'That's Prince Charles,' I hear on the radio. 'They will be coming past you in just a few minutes.' By now, I'm not tired at all and enjoying myself immensely.

I reverse the 4×4 off the track and up through the trees: it's steep but quite dry. I stop just as I see the ghillie cresting the hill – and he's got the stag harnessed up. I jump out of the Landy, run up the hill and help the last few hundred yards. We haul the carcass into the back, just as an advance party of squaddies comes past. 'That's the Prince's security detail,' the ghillie says, grinning but looking mightily relieved. 'We only just made it.'

A day or two later, when I'm still congratulating myself we didn't get caught, I'm out walking the dog when I bump into the owner of the estate we're renting from. He's staying in a lodge down the drive, whilst we've taken up residence in the baronial pile that's his by rights. Still, he seems pleased to see me.

'I hear you poached a stag from the Queen,' he says by way of an opener. Up until then, I'd kept quiet about our shenanigans, not wanting to get our young ghillie into trouble (or my own hands cut off, being sent to the colonies ...) However, the cat seems out of the bag, so I nod.

'Yes,' I reply and do my best to look sorry. 'I hope it doesn't get you into trouble?'

'Oh, I doubt that,' replies our host, his brow unfurrowed. 'Funnily enough, I did the same thing in exactly the same spot a few years ago.'

'Oh?'

'Probably a bit like you, I walked around for a few days, grappling with my conscience, then I wrote to Her Majesty and apologised.'

'What happened?'

'Well, it all turned out for the best,' he replied, smiling. 'She wrote back almost immediately, insisting it wasn't a problem and invited me for a day's grouse shooting.'

August
GROUSE,
THE ART OF WALKED UP SHOOTING
AND THE IMPORTANCE OF
NEVER TUCKING YOUR
WATERPROOF TROUSERS INTO YOUR BOOTS

I'd always assumed that most forms of hunting, shooting or fishing in Scotland had a sort of Hills & Heather premium attached: basically, the same as Down South but twenty percent extra for the amazing backdrop.

I think that if you're also central heating a castle or two, then making the most of rural Scotland is expensive ... but it doesn't have to be. Rent. If there are more than about twelve of you (including kids), then a nice Scottish house, somewhere between a big parsonage and a small castle will set everyone back less than a bunch of hotel rooms and you get your own chef and a housekeeper to boss you about. There will be cooked breakfasts, packed lunches for those who are dispersing to engage in healthy outdoor activities, tea in the drawing room at 4pm (with cake), drinks over snooker and game in the evening.

The sport is cheap-ish, too. For example, I'm standing on a grouse moor with every intention of shooting some privately-educated grouse and it's costing less than a normal day's shooting in Oxfordshire. Expensive, but I don't need to wonder which of my organs would fetch the most on the Dark Web.

Good value might have something to do with the fact we

parked the cars a vertical mile away then took a fully laden Argo up what was essentially a cliff with bobbles and the occasional tuft of heather. These things will go anywhere, they're like the buggies you always wanted when you were a kid. However, the humans, assorted dogs, shotguns and cartridges inside are still very much subject to the laws of gravity and holding on for dear life without bursting into tears is the priority for the next ten minutes. The driver is strapped in, so he's was having a ball.

Finally, up top and once my heart rate returns to normal, I can appreciate the view, which is similar to what you get about three minutes after take-off. A huge, tumbling sky with broken, slate-coloured clouds, and glimpses of blue behind is counter-weighted by broad, sweeping hills. Puffs of white mist hover above clumps of grass and heather that tumble down to a loch, which is reflecting the whole vista back, like one of those eternal mirrors.

It starts to rain in earnest as we arrive at our start point, which just serves to make the ghillie and his team of beaters and dogs look even more dour, as if all this weather is our fault. They haven't really said very much to us, at all, but it was fairly obvious how unimpressed they were when, at 9am, up rolled in an assortment of expensive and rather too-clean-for-their-taste 4×4s, out of which tumbled children, wives and a bunch of English toffs.

That's not strictly true: there's several nationalities in our party and everyone, as far as I know, has worked their arse off to afford the big cars, the day's shooting and eye-wateringly ex-pensive wellies – but the whole beater-gun divide in shooting creates a palpable Us & Them vibe sometimes. Well, often.

It's in these slightly unpromising circumstances that the shoot starts.

'Walked up' shooting is a pretty straightforward proposition: You spread out in a line and you walk until there is something to shoot at. It is probably my favourite way of shooting anything – whether I'm going out alone, with a dog or with a whole bunch of people – half of whom think I'm a bit of a twit.

In reality, teetering on top of a Scottish hill, in the driving rain, it isn't that simple. Firstly, the dogs all feel they had been very patient up until now: they'd been turfed out of bed early, seen lots of guns, muddy boots and heard lots of their favourite words, yet the humans are still faffing about instead of racing across the heather.

I've always thought that keeping them off a lead so they can put birds up, but close enough so the birds are not out of range – dark, diminishing specs on the horizon – is one of the hardest training tricks to master. A dog wants to go off into the middle distance, a shotgun is only really effective at about fifty yards: time and patience is the difference between the two.

On top of this, most guns and beaters have dogs not just of differing abilities but breeds: willing-enough but largely apathetic labradors do their best to politely ignore the ADHD spaniels and there's nearly always a pointer or two that will point at everything and nothing including comely bushes and bees.

Secondly, having one leg a foot higher than the other thanks to the forty-five-degree angle, the clumps of heather and all the pointy rocks the clumps of heather are concealing, mean the line breaks repeatedly as someone unexpectedly disappears from view, then bounces up again a few seconds later, hopefully with their gun pointing somewhere everyone else isn't.

As we set off a couple of hares get up from under our feet and gallop away. Being 'ground' game on a bird day, they obviously aren't for taking pot shots at – but I'd find it hard to shoot them, anyway: I come from a part of the world where hares are such a rarity that you stop the car to watch them jinking about in fields. Today, they are everywhere, which drives the dogs mad and proves quite disconcerting for us – a bit like nineteenth century guns having to deal with flocks of parrots they are strictly forbidden from shooting.

Which probably explains why we miss the first grouse that breaks cover and arcs off into the murky distance. Then the second.

Nothing to panic about but I know what everyone must be thinking. The previous year, further north, near Ullapool the same group of friends had spent three days tramping about the Highlands to shoot one solitary grouse. That's a good fifteen to twenty hours wandering about in wellies and weather with very little to show for it. Lovely place to be, but ...

So, when we watch our second bird glide across the undulating terrain, downwards to the safety of the loch, we do wonder if it could have been our last.

Shooting things going away from you, especially when you're stumbling along at an odd angle, I've always found harder than it looks. All game shooting is, I suppose. When you assume a pellet spread of two or more feet over thirty odd yards, you'd think it would be tough – nigh on impossible – to miss anything, even if you tried quite hard. However, all of us know, from bitter experience, that it is the norm to watch your quarry flying off in the best of health after you've pulled the trigger. Even on a relatively good day, our lot only average about a thirty to fifty percent kill rate – much less if we've got hangovers or the birds are a bit high, or it's windy.

However, a bird flying away from you, should surely just be a straight aim and shoot? I think you have to factor in adrenaline (i.e. surprise when this small brown thing suddenly bursts out of a clump of something in front of you just as your mind had started to wander or you were shouting at the dog), more adrenaline when you realise it's a safe shot and it's yours (i.e. it doesn't try and fly behind you and therefore shouldn't be shot at for safety reasons, namely the necessity of swinging your gun around and pointing it – albeit briefly – at your friends and family). Then there is the fact that things never fly completely straight: birds tend to rise, then dip and bank right or left in a trajectory your rain-slippery gun has to follow to stand any chance.

That said, like a lot of us, I find it's best not to think about all that and let muscle memory take over. So, forget the geometry and give your balance, articulation and movement over to whatever prehistoric nodules in our brain might still exist; even after the twentieth century onwards has done its best to eradicate intuition in favour of science.

And this is why walked up, 'snap shooting' is such a pleasure. Shooting a moving target by instinct feels right – righter – than the measured, more formal versions.

And humans have this knack for getting in sync. Bit by bit, and as the wind blows off some of the rain, the line becomes less ragged, and the dogs settle.

When the third grouse breaks from where it was hiding in a familiar thrum of small wing beats, the nearest gun is sufficiently poised to pick the right range and angle. One shot rings out across the spacious valley and the bird tumbles out of the sky to be retrieved by one of the dogs who is probably just as relieved as we are.

And we are off.

The hares bolting at our feet cease to bother as they slice through the heather, and nor do we pay the weather much mind as it blusters above our heads.

With a frequency that feels increasingly like a rhythm, birds bolt, away from our tramping and the tally ticks up to double figures.

The weather steadily improves, the sky churning blue and white with a stray black cloud, here and there – like Italian marble, shot with streaks of sun that doesn't quite warm but is welcome enough.

Suddenly it feels less like a slog, more like honest work.

We stop for lunch in a bothy – probably more memorable for the fact it had a fire we can dry off next to. Our two boys had made the rookie error of tucking their wet weather trousers into their boots, which had filled with water, so wellies are emptied, socks wrung out, then left to hang where they can at least warm up. In a couple of years, these two will be shooting alongside us but, for now, this is still new enough to be exciting and, like most boys, feeling like you're part of the team is the half of it.

After lunch we circle back to do a sweep of the lower portion of the hill. The birds keep coming – neither in flocks or as rarities, just a steady supply, one every five or ten minutes.

And at the end of the day, exhausted, we hobble off the hill, back to the stone house next to where the cars were parked. We have around twenty-five birds, which worked out at three or four each over about ten kilometres: too much, I daresay, for people who aren't fans, not nearly enough for ardent grouse guns, who are probably more enthusiastic about butts where the birds sweep fast and low over the heather in squadrons. There, the bag rises as your bank balance plummets, like a barometer in the jaws of a blizzard.

Either way, quite enough for four families. A few days later I would joint and fillet them in the pantry of the house where we were staying ... and we would gobble them up with braised cabbage, celeriac purée and sauce Albert.

Right now, we are just pleased to put our feet up by the fire and chat about the day with each other, the beaters and the ghillie. As soon as I sit down, I'm handed a wee dram of scotch, which filled a good half of the tumbler.

They like us now, even with our English accents, breeks, silly socks and too-big cars. We'd shot OK, the kids had been stalwarts and no-one's dog had bounded off and spoiled the drive.

It proved a point: walked up shooting is the great leveller, it brings beaters, guns, dogs and small boys together, because you're all in it together, hauling yourself across the same terrain and watching the day unfurl from the same perspective. Unlike driven shooting, which sometimes feels you're marching towards one another, on opposite sides.

When it's all over, trying to dry your clothes by the same fire as the whisky burns your throat, fires your veins and loosens your tongue. Talking shit about great feats that may or may not deserve to be feted, surrounded by friends, family and doggies is as good as it gets.

Because of the way it unfolded, because of the place and, most of all, because of the people who shared it, makes that day, high up on a rainy hill in Scotland, one of the best day's shooting I've ever had.

September
TREEHOUSES, GUNS AND ALCOHOL

Nine hundred miles away, across the Channel, it's a bit different. Again.

Today, I've been invited by some locals *à la chasse aux palombes* – migrating pigeons that move south towards Spain in huge flocks. I've seen over a thousand in one mass, preceded by a disconcerting whispering of feathers beating frozen air.

However, shooting a pigeon whilst it is flying by is considered very bad form in France – this is the opposite of the UK, where you are generally considered a cad of the first order if you do anything less. Around us in France, shooting a *palombe* on the wing will get you drummed out of Le Club des Chasseurs. This has nothing to do with shoes – for those of you whose French is rusty; in France, a *chasseur* translates as *a man in very old clothes who gets dangerously pissed whilst armed.*

Nevertheless, even twatted to the point you cannot stand up, there is still very little chance of going away empty-handed, as the French method requires almost no ability at firing a gun, save for remembering to stand at the right end of it when you pull the trigger.

I've been a few times since and it is one of those activities where you tell yourself, never again. Until the memory fades and, like childbirth, seaside holidays in north Wales or bungee jumping, and you just remember the good bits before deciding, what the heck.

My first day of *la chasse aux palombes* went something like this:

Woke very early. Lift, in a pickup, to a wood. Deeply concerned I will never be heard from again. In the car, I am offered a hip flask. Bit early; but if I am to be raped by French rednecks and buried in a shallow grave, I might as well get a drink out of it. The plum *eau de vie* strips the first three layers of skin from the roof of my mouth and makes my teeth hurt.

Arrive at spot in wood where we are met by more scary men wearing what look like green bin liners attached to their bodies with binder twine. They are carrying some of the oldest shot-guns I have ever seen not on someone's mantelpiece. Am handed a generous lump of *saucisson*, some bread and more of that moonshine. Worryingly, I'm beginning to acclimatise to the taste. Someone lends me a rusty gun that weighs more than my leg.

Feeling less anxious, warm and slightly pissed, we make our way to the hide.

I look up at it. I blink.

It's hard to describe what I am seeing: those houses on stilts in Asian fishing villages are as close as I can get ... except, instead of hovering above a blue-green lagoon, these are substantial huts that are about forty-seven feet up a tree, connected by a series of gantries that are basically homemade ladders lashed together with the same stuff they are using to stop their trousers falling down.

The men grin and nod at me encouragingly and I start to feel nervous again.

I am shown a ladder that goes up to the largest cabin on stilts and invited to climb it. I take another swig of the plum drink and race up – before I change my mind and dash off into the woods.

The interior is surprisingly well-equipped and, within ten minutes, a stove is lit and we're all very cosy. But not too cosy, thankfully.

Somebody produces some beer and I tuck in.

I've noticed that one of the hunters has stayed below, and I watch from a small window as he goes to a cage and brings out a live pigeon. He attaches his pet bird to a miniature platform.

'What's that?' I ask one of the guns.

'That's the *piège*,' (decoy), he replies.

'Oh,' I say, surprised and admiring, 'in England we use plastic pigeons for decoys.' He stares wordlessly at me, as if I'd just said, *We English dangle our willies out of our trousers to attract birds*.

I smile weakly and get up to help myself to another beer. The plum stuff was incredibly strong, and on a mainly empty stomach, and I'm feeling properly pissed now.

By the looks of things so is everyone else and the atmosphere in the fuggish hut right up here in the tree is cheery, without there being much by way of actual talking. There is some grunting, whereupon most of the guys pull various packets of food out of their bags and trouser pockets.

Lunch or *branch* (brunch up a tree) is clearly a lot more important than shooting, so it's just me who watches the decoy pigeon's platform being raised on a sort of mini winch.

The pigeon, attached by leather jesses, looks out of sorts as it is hoisted slowly to the top of the canopy that is at least another thirty feet above our heads. Can't say I blame it. Job done, the pigeon man goes back to the cage and brings another pigeon out. He repeats the process three or four times until we have a good spread of decoys about forty feet from the hut (no distance at all, in shooting terms). Then he climbs up the ladder, winks at me and asks about food.

Shooting still seems very much off the agenda (much to the decoys' relief, who are all up their trees doing the pigeon equivalent of saying 'Faaaarrckiing hell...' under their breaths as they wave about in the breeze a short distance from a lot of pissed men with guns).

Food seems to be coming along nicely and I'm poured a very large glass of red wine and offered some more *saucisson*, neither of which touches the sides as it goes down. I'm famished and now completely accepting of the fact that this is really just an elaborate drinking contest.

But the hot food, when it comes, is also delicious. These guys have produced fresh steaks with all the trimmings – sautéed potatoes, vegetable gratin and tomato salad – on a stove you'd normally use for making a cup of tea by the side of the A303.

The wine is excellent, too: rough, but in a good way, it cuts through the grease but goes down well because, underneath the tannins, it's perfectly balanced.

Unlike me.

We are mopping up juices with more bread and someone is getting out the cheese when there's a shout and everyone puts their plates down and picks up the nearest gun.

It seems the decoys have done their job and the air above the canopy of bare trees is full – utterly blue-grey – with pigeons. The flock must be made up of something like three hundred birds, and it wheels and turns above our heads almost like those swarms of swifts that roost under bridges in London.

Our decoys now are properly agitated. I can almost imagine one or two of the 'free' birds wheeling about overhead saying to the rest of them, 'Look, there's Dave, and he's sitting in a tree... Dave! Dave! Daaaaave!! Dave.Dave.Dave.Dave.Dave.Dave... Daaaaaaaaavvvvvvve! ... Ah, fuck it, let's go down and see what he's doing.' Whilst Decoy Dave is frantically trying to shoo them away:

'You really don't want to come down here – there's men and they're armed to the teeth.'

'Bollocks,' his friends say, 'you're probably just stuffing your face. We're coming down.'

And come down they did. Several hundred in the trees all around us.

Within seconds the sky was filled with lead as Frenchmen pick a spot in the trees above and let rip. There are so many birds, you can't miss, and what's more they keep flying up then coming back.

For about five minutes it's mayhem. It feels a bit like the final scene in *Zulu* and my ears are ringing when somebody finally calls time, and we all stop and peer over the side of our airborne Wendy house.

At the base of the trees there must be over one hundred dead or flapping pigeons.

'*Très bon,*' they grunt and go back to their cheese course.

October

WILD BOAR,
WHY YOU SHOULD NEVER DRIVE A TRACTOR
NEAR A SHOOT IN FRANCE
AND THE BRILLIANCE OF BOAR HOUNDS

I'm loitering about another shooting ground in South-western France.

I've switched hilly woodland for a discreet valley with exuberant hedgerow and soft grass. October here is still very much summer with a second growth coming a month before, like another bite of the cherry. A narrow river – one that started life as snowmelt from the Pyrenees – snakes through a field splashed with poppies and fringed with attractive cornflower.

A small but significant part of the river is going into my wellies. Even in the height of summer, these ice-fed streams and brooks make your bones ache.

We're arguing whilst an injured boar close by drowns noisily. It's just out of reach.

'My cousin farms just up the hill, he's got waders.'

'So what? I'm still not going near that thing until it's good and dead.'

'What about a fishing rod?'

'Didn't you hear me first time?'

'Shoot it again, at least.'

This relatively sensible (and humane) suggestion meets with grunts of approval, but no-one does anything.

This is shooting at the brutal end of the scale, by farmers and retired labourers who do it because wild boar damage crops, so need to be kept in check – plus they are delicious.

I'm pretty sure the only reason I'm invited is because my rifle is at least fifty years newer than anything they lug about. I've also got all my own limbs, sight in both eyes and can manage more than a brisk shamble.

Which is why I sometimes get up at 6am on a Saturday to follow their battered 2CVs and Peugeot vans in my British Mini Countryman, whilst they get grumpier and more murderous as the day unfolds. They start drinking at 7am – gut rot wine and baguette, they're drunk by nine and hungover by elevenses, which is about when I usually make my excuses.

In nearly ten years no-one has asked me where I'm from or sometimes even bothered to speak to me in French. The language of shooting around here is the local Gascon, *Béarnaise*: a sing-song cross between French and Spanish, with a bit of Basque shouldering in by way of the odd noun, just to make its presence felt.

Aside from the drinking and the fact nearly all of them should be banned from shooting because they're blood-thirsty and senile, I have to admit to a grudging respect for these tooled-up octogenarians that has built up over the years and is the reason why I still turn up.

Wild boars are tough, clever and very dangerous.

Slightly brighter than a very bright dog, they've got the ability to blend into either brush, woodland or crop in a way that is astonishing, then alarming when they do materialise and shoot off with a turn of speed you'd normally attribute to a reasonably-priced motorbike. They've also got a pair of tusks it's no exaggeration to say you could give yourself a half decent shave with.

So, they're big, angry pigs who aren't overly scared of us or the dogs we use.

But, sometimes, they pretend to be, such is their sneakiness. I've known a boar to 'take fright' and dash off into woodland, followed by a baying pack of dogs. Then hide behind a tree, wait for the dogs to pass, jump out and gut the dog making up the tail end.

They kill humans, too – aside from thousands of car accidents they cause annually in Europe, a significant number of people do get attacked whilst innocently walking about in the countryside, which is not surprising when boar numbers are on the rise to such a degree. According to the French government website, the last couple of decades of warmer winters, lack of any natural predators and Covid (though they don't explain that one) has seen a twenty-fold increase in boar to about two million. The number of them killed annually in France has kept pace: up from around forty thousand a year in the early 1970s to eight hundred thousand in 2021, which leads me to suspect that bits of wild piggy must surely be getting into ready meals and eaten by an unsuspecting public whether they like it or not. It's a huge amount but that still leaves over a million running about eating and shagging. And that's a lot for a relatively built-up country.

And they do get everywhere: around us they've made it into most parts of town, including the airport (I received a breathless call from someone I play football with late one Sunday evening to come and shoot it [I declined on the reasonable basis that guns and airports don't mix for private citizens]). And they've even popped into the reception area of the local hospital.

In parts of Europe there are worrying signs that wild boar are losing the ability to forage for themselves and have come to rely on humans for sustenance, like urban foxes in London. In Germany, one nicknamed Elsa, was responsible for gate crashing a child's birthday party, scoffing the cake and helping herself to most of the treat bags, before disappearing to sleep off the sugar rush in the local forest. Sometimes the attacks seem as malevolent as they are for the practical necessity of eating: the previous week the very same boar was filmed stealing the laptop of a naturist bather, who became a predictable YouTube star by entertaining millions of bored social media users as he scampered about after Elsa in the buff.

And whilst my fellow hunters are good countrymen all – who go out a couple of times a week and risk what little remains of their own lifespans and appendages – I'm most impressed by the dogs.

I'm used to working dogs being quite closely defined by their job. So, ratters have to be small, wiery and angry at the world in general, which they then take it out on rodents – hence a terrier of some description. A peg dog needs to be composed (possibly a tad lazy), with an oral fixation and easy to train because their owner is busy running a bank or bringing up a family, so it has to be a lab. And a springer as your dog choice on the beating line is hard to better because they act like they are on speed but really, they just want to please you and I've rarely met a dog with a sense of smell as good or an enthusiasm for driven birds as astonishing. But there doesn't seem to be a 'boar dog' per se: they're all pretty big, quite shaggy and extremely vocal ... and that's about it. Some are huge, like small, unshod ponies and others just look a bit like sheepdogs crossed with something that's been to the gym. But one thing they have in common in my experience is none of them are interested in us humans: they've got a job to do, which is to leap out of the back of a rickety car and shoot off after anything that smells slightly boary.

These are definitely not the wagging-tailed-pleased-to-see-everyone labs and springers of genteel English Home Counties driven shoots: if you come across one on a drive, they'll stop for long enough to see if you have anything to say for yourself, then push past you. Stroking them is like patting a lump of mahogany covered in pelt. They have to be focused and fit. Quite frankly, I find it hard enough to train a decent gundog to concentrate for the duration of two hundred yards of a drive, yet these boar hounds are on a different level on pack instinct alone: regularly doing five-to-ten-mile beats under their own steam and initiative.

At the start of a drive, they are dropped off, then tracked either by all of us lot listening to their baying from a safe distance, or by their owner squinting at their mobile, following their collar trackers as they tear through woods, across fields, along valleys and down busy roads – the latter a bit more often than anyone would like. Their tones change when they latch onto a scent, going up another octave when they get sight of a boar, which will (usually) run from them ... and towards us. There's quite a lot of France between the dogs and us to start with and there may be ramblers or cyclists along the way – so you can see where the risk to the general public lies in all of this hoo ha.

As is usually the case, the men with guns have got the easy job: we've got cars. All we have to do is drive to where we think they'll all end up, given the direction our ears tell us they are going and hopefully shoot the boar when it pops up.

Considering the amount rough ground the dogs have to cover, it's always slightly amazing that – with one or two exceptions – they all arrive at the end of a two hour drive more or less where we expect them to be. No-one has sent them on expensive training courses and nor are they the product of somewhat inhumane breeding practices in pursuit of the ideal boar hound. They're united under a common flag: to bound after something big and dangerous because it runs away (most of the time).

This is a long-winded way of stating that I happen to think that the best bit of any field sport you can do is work with dogs.

Which is why I felt quite aggrieved when a man comes over to me one day whilst I'm out shooting boar and says, 'What do you think you're playing at?'

His tone makes me do a little jump on the spot, a bit like Bertie Wooster being caught on a landing doing something unwise. That and the fact he's appeared from nowhere – seemingly corkscrewing out of the ground or by falling out of a tree.

I've been posted at the southern flank of the drive, at the edge of a spinney overlooking a few *bijoux* fields grouped at the edge of one giant one. It's a bit of a climb to where I am leaning up against a large oak, listening to the ebb and flow of the hounds' progress, so the old boy is showing an admirable degree of motivation.

Nevertheless, even from twenty yards, I don't like the look of him. He looks crabby.

'I said, "what are you doing?".'

'I'm shooting *sangliers*. Go away.' I say it in French, but I'm half tempted to speak English as it's the quickest route to ending a conversation I'm already sure I don't want to have.

I'm not habitually rude and I think my resting face is relatively friendly, so he's momentarily taken aback. He straightens his back and recalibrates.

'Yes, but you're facing the wrong way!'

'No, I'm not. If the boar tries to break left, he'll have to cross that wood and he'll appear from there!' I point at the edge of the wood where a grassy field starts. It's ideal, I've got a good view, and any stray shells will go into the ground because I'm shooting at a nice and safe downward angle.

'Yes, but the dogs will be behind the pig, you might shoot one of them.'

This is very unfair, I've been shooting long enough not to shoot into anything I don't have a decent line of sight through (woods, thickets) or at anything that isn't game (mountain bikers, vicars on bikes, lorries carrying fuel ... *and* dogs). Out of all of the above, I like dogs the best. But I keep my cool.

'Where would you have me shoot, old man?'

'There.' He points a large, bony finger in the direction of the biggest field where, I've neglected to mention, a man in a tractor is ploughing up maize stubble.

Now, this might be a just-about-by-the-seat-of-ones-breeks safe shot if I was shooting solid rounds through a shotgun. They are illegal in the UK but a very useful cartridge in France – essentially like shooting a sharpened musket ball through your trusty twelve bore. It's deadly up to around thirty or forty yards but after that the slug starts to tumble and drop. Personally, I think they're the best way to shoot boar as one of these will knock it sideways or miss and become harmless very quickly. This is the ballistic opposite of my horrible plastic Weatherby .258 with its military grade shells. The tiny, pointed slug on top makes it look like a stupid .303 shell that failed the army entrance board: all the muscle but with a tiny head on its shoulders. I wish I'd never bought this rifle because it looks like something to be used in a mass killing. It unnerves me – and for good reason, if I miss and the bullet is able to carry on travelling unhindered, it can still kill someone putting out their washing almost a mile away.

Firing a rifle anywhere near a man in a tractor is such a stupid suggestion, I should just wander off. Instead, I point at the farmer ploughing his field. 'What about him?' I ask, already knowing I'm not going to like the answer.

'You can shoot *around* him,' he insists, as if it is the most obvious thing in all the world.

I assume the old man knows his shooting, so he can see that I'm carrying a high-powered weapon – if only by virtue of the fact my Weatherby has the sort of scope fitted you generally only see in films where someone is trying to kill the American President from very far away. This doesn't seem to worry him, which is sort of par for the course in this part of the world, where I've had a loaded weapon pointed at me on more than one occasion as someone has swung through the line, tracking a running boar.

Accidents are going down. A bit. Looking online there are around one hundred incidents involving French people out hunting (i.e., someone gets shot) and around eight fatalities a year, which is A LOT (statistics for the same in the UK point at well under half that number of fatalities and nothing close to that number of lesser injuries).

This is a very real problem, and the hunting fraternity gets deservedly bad press. However, if they could clean up their act in respect of booze and basic safety, they should get the credit they deserve for generally being a good thing – essentially doing the government and farmers' jobs by culling animals that destroy crops and cause a great many serious accidents on roads.

So, this is one reason why I still do it. The other is for the shoot lunch that comes around but once a year.

Like the shooting itself in France, this event on the gallic shooting calendar is virtually free. Or a heck of a lot cheaper than its UK counterpart. At the time of writing this masterpiece, a day's driven shooting in the Home Counties, with driven pheasant or partridge or a bit of both, lots to eat and a something to drink will set you back the price of a cheap second-hand car, or an expensive double case of champagne ... or one hundred and forty-two pints of beer, according to the calculator on my phone.

A *day*.

But then there's the accessories: by way of example, a pair of breeks (plus fours) – which aren't even a whole trouser – is about a hundred quid at the starter level (which would be the shooting equivalent of going to Primark) and you can only wear breeks when you leave the house to go driven shooting. In any other situation, except perhaps amateur dramatics, you'll look a fool. And you can't possibly wear normal socks either, you have to spend sixty quid on garish woolly ones, anything up to £800 for a coat and a pair of wellies with a zip up the side (another essential/non-essential) is three hundred quid. Finally, when it's all over, as you get handed just two of the fifteen or so birds you shot, you have to dish out a forty-pound tip to the keeper – just in case you're not already impoverished enough.

Around us in Aquitaine I pay a whisker over a hundred euros for shooting rights that span just under forty thousand hectares and, as long as I'm wearing a high vis jacket and not, otherwise, naked, I'm good to go.

To be fair, there's probably more to shoot in your average five-acre field in England and a bit of wood than over a dozen kilometres of real estate in France, partly because plastered Frenchmen have shot everything in the 1970s but also because we chronically overstock in the UK. As is often the case, somewhere in between would be better for everyone either side of the channel.

But here, profoundly in Southwestern France, the food that is costing me almost nothing to make dead, then cook, then eat, is well worth arguing with octogenarians and risking my life on a semi-regular basis.

The Salle des Fêtes in our small village with its stone flooring, warped tables and wooden benches fills up to resemble something out of the final, double page spread in *Asterix*. Farmers and retired farmers mingle, and the talk is all tractors.

Or wild piggies.

If you can't wax on about these old foes in mixed tones of respect, animosity and affection, then you'll struggle to get through even the first course.

Partially, also because it's always cabbage soup.

'Garbure' is what I imagine Charlie Bucket and his family lived off, except at least it's got tasty lumps of bacon in it and the stock is light enough to pique hunger, yet salty enough to round off your cold beer satisfyingly. That done, you grab the red wine carafe as it sails past and wait for the next course.

The wine is bought in bulk, for less than the cost of a pint of milk and should, by all rights, be a bit grim but somehow nearly always turns out to be light and extremely easy to drink. Too easy, because I've usually had more than my fair share before the second course arrives in the form of thinly-sliced venison steaks and gratin dauphinoise à la industrial scale. There's one weekend a year where I quickly learned the whole of Aquitaine is mobilised to go and cull deer instead of mowing the lawn or clean the car. It's frantic but efficient species control and it does mean that the deer are left alone for the rest of the year to roam about looking elegant, doing whatever deer do.

Growing up, I wasn't much of a fan of venison: most of the cuts put in front of me came in a thick, red-fruity sauce that was too boozey for my nine-year-old tastes and the meat smelled of old socks with a slightly too-sweet aroma of decay.

Hung for just the right amount of time, and cooked like any normal protein, venison has all the satisfying sinew of beef and the just-so gaminess of lamb.

You don't want to stuff your face, though, because the main event starts to fan out down the long tables about now. Miniature mountains of oven-warm bread, piled up in baskets is carried in alongside triumphant-looking platters of marinaded boar ribs. More wine is sloshed into plastic beakers, and we get stuck in.

It really does get very *Asterix* at this juncture, as piles of stripped bones are tossed aside to make way for ribs fresh off the barbecue.

Of course, after sucking the hot succulent flesh off half a dozen ribs each, we're all still weak with hunger, so we have to have cheese, followed by something sweet and sticky, coffee and a generous Armagnac to make sure you can digest it.

Then we all have enemas!

OK, perhaps I'm exaggerating – not EVERYONE goes for Armagnac and quite a few of the older guns have expired from old age before the cheese course.

However, it is the perfect way to lose three quarters of a day and to make up for all those times you spend standing in a field for six hours freezing your nuts off, waiting for a boar that never comes. Or fearing for your life when it does and everyone opens fire from several intersecting angles that were not agreed because everyone has a much better idea where they should be, other than where they were posted originally.

Gallic boar hunting is chaotic, ungentlemanly and a little bit lethal. But, thanks to the exploding population of wild piggies up and down the country, it has never been so necessary whilst never being so much in need of reform. Change it must but, in certain respects, I hope not too much.

November

DRIVEN SHOOTING, REFLECTIONS ON SOMERSET AND HOW THE PEN IS MIGHTIER THAN THE SWORD ... ESPECIALLY WHEN IT COMES TO COWS.

Far away the from mad chases and cheese courses of France, I'm knocking about on the edge of the Mendips in Somerset.

God it's damp.

If you stand about in a wet field for long enough, you start to be able to distinguish between the different smells of wet mud, wet grass, wet hawthorn and wet spaniel. In this respect, driven shooting is educational.

Then again, standing still, in silence – anywhere – is enlightening.

For the last five minutes before the actual shooting bit of any drive, there's a sense of something between trepidation and high hopes: the beaters close in, like an advancing line of Buffs, sticks beat the grass and dogs punch through the brambles as some of the more nervous birds make a break for it. Then guns snap shut, and the blood rushes a little faster through head and heart. For a good twenty minutes before all of this, though, I often wish I still smoked. Or I'd brought a book.

Today, I've got something else to take my mind off the dead time between the guns getting in place and the beaters slowly covering the broken ground, across cover crop, corn stubble and coppice.

I'm back within half a mile or so of where I wound up at school between the ages of thirteen and eighteen. Downside Abbey, whose shadow loomed over me most days for five years, sits on the grim brow of the horizon: stodgy and square, like an ecclesiastical privy.

That's actually a bit unfair: somewhere else it could be truly beautiful, somewhere the sun shone more often – as part of a former city state in France or Northern Italy, its blockishness diluted by quainter buildings. Here it's too heavy to be elegant – in the way that Salisbury Cathedral achieves – and not well enough sited amongst parkland to be truly grandiose – like Blenheim.

But for five highly formative years I called it home, and the friends I made there are more like family today. We squabbled through boyhood and adolescence – from dormitory to study, sports pitch to pub; regrouped after university in shared hovels; drank through the London Years (as paupers, at first, then with cash to burn); settled down to marry; and became godparents to children who miraculously get on as their parents did.

With my friends I know I am very lucky. And very grateful.

Coming back to this rainy corner of Somerset twice a year to blow unfortunate poultry out of the sky feels a bit like coming home.

But it wasn't always like that.

Doubtless I had been lucky up until Downside – my small prep school had been a cosier place, nestling in the gentle Oxfordshire countryside I was familiar with – here it was the wilds of the Mendips: brooding cows and driving rain.

And talking of cows ...

At twelve, I had been greatly looking forward to going to my new school and becoming an officer cadet. That was until I joined in my first term and quickly realised it mainly involved a lot of waiting around for the minibus and pointless runs.

This wasn't too much of a problem, having several years at boarding school under our belts by way of prep school from seven to twelve, most of us were virtuoso shirkers. *Dad's Army* had nothing on us in the Downside CCF. Whilst giving every semblance of keen application, we fumbled rifles dangerously, tore maps, contrived to misunderstand the simplest instructions and generally fucked about until the officers in charge gave up and we found ourselves in a classroom being shown safety videos. Sometimes they exacted their revenge by giving us long lectures on radio waves or gun cleaning, but we didn't mind – at least it was warm and dry inside.

However, once a year we went on exercise. And this was our opportunity to really shine.

The usual drill went like this: bussed, en masse, up onto the windswept Mendips, we were handed ancient Lee-Enfields that hadn't changed in basic design since the First World War. We were given some army rations, three blank rounds and told to go and pretend to kill one another.

As soon as we were given our orders, it was absolutely essential to get as far away from the 'commanding officers' as quickly as possible and hide. You only came back when you saw the coaches draw up in the car park as it began to get dark. Hanging about was madness – although probably a lot less mad and disorganised than actual war, where running away and hiding is also an option, albeit one that will get you shot as opposed to a Wednesday detention.

We all knew that the annual exercise was simply an excuse for the older boys to muster the third formers into private armies to fight each other – it was basically Afghanistan under a system of warlords... but in Somerset. To avoid becoming cannon fodder in a prefect's turf war, we legged it.

The second thing to know is that whilst a blank round does not actually have a bullet, it can do a surprising amount of damage at close range. The wadding comes out as a plug of paper, and there would be boys emerging from bushes with it in their hair, like smouldering confetti, complaining, adenoidally, that they had gone deaf.

However, a Spanish kid went one better and shot at a cow. First, he put a lead pencil down the barrel. To everyone's surprise and consternation, including and especially the cow's, the pencil killed it.

I can't remember what eventually happened to the boy, except we were all quite surprised when he wasn't expelled. Quips along the lines of *goes to show, sir, the pen is mightier than the sword, sir!* were met with stern looks, but if there's one thing I learned about public school, you never took anything seriously – even dead cows shot with HBs.

I was sticking it out because I had every intention of joining the army. Plus, if you're British, you're always going to be persuadable to get involved in any activity that involves dressing up.

And that's what I've been thinking about today, in between drives, because there's more than a hint of the nostalgia and escapism I craved back then in the CCF with its caps, putties and Lee Enfields as there is with the formal, driven shooting that I'm doing right now.

The whole dressing up thing, I mentioned in an earlier chapter, really is pretty central to this: tweed, leather and woolly stuff is the order of the day for the most part. And ties. It's probably the only time I wear one these days outside of death, marriage and court appearances. Done right, as you step out of your front door, you need to be looking like a cross between Rupert the Bear and John McCririck or you're just not doing it right. It's easy to scoff, but weekend cyclists, yoga mums, tots in Messi shirts, High Court Judges, Batman ... everyone needs a uniform, or it doesn't feel right. And the more outlandish, the better – you know, to distinguish what you are doing from someone who's just popped to the shops.

If all the disguising yourself as a 1920s landowner isn't enough, then there are other traditions I like. The day nearly always starts in some country pile you wouldn't normally get near unless it was part of the National Trust and then you'd have to queue up for a slightly sad Ploughman's in some purpose-built annexe, instead of stomping up to the main house for hot coffee and bacon rolls. There's always one or two people about to make you feel welcome and a bit important, then a game-keeper and beaters to make you feel the opposite. There are good dogs, bad dogs, eccentric gun buses to drive you about that started life eighty years before as a Red Cross Ambulance in Normandy or a railway carriage and an even more eccentric landowner who might or might not surface with a wreck of a labrador in tow just as champagne, sloe gin and bits of pheasant on a stick are being served for elevenses.

As far as I'm concerned, there's nothing not to like here.

In all of this, however, there is the difficulty of shooting seemingly laughably easy birds that are flying towards you whilst everyone is watching.

Personally, I always find that the problem with the beating line in front and birds essentially flying right at you is *time*. Too much of it. If the build-up between spotting an over-fed pheasant flapping laboriously over the horizon and it eventually reaching you is long enough to wrap up a phone call to your mum, straighten your hat, adjust your flies and check who's watching, then you'll miss eleven times out of ten. Well, I will, anyway.

When I was younger, it was all too easy, now my heart tends to sink when I see a pheasant or partridge approaching head on. I'll either have to take it caddishly early or hope that one of my so-called friends poaches it.

It tends to be fine when a drive hots up and the birds start coming thick and fast, when tracking and lead start to be natural, rather than over-thought and a bit fraught by conflict-ing theories and guesswork. I do find the old adage of pretend-ing the gun is a hosepipe and you're trying to drench the bird in a fluid, continuous movement does work but more so with 'crossers' (left to right, better, I find, right to left, best – don't ask me why).

There are rare days when I think I've cracked it, when I find my timing and range and it's back to being easy again and then

I think to myself that I just need to recall that feeling each time I shoulder a gun and it will be the same. Tweedy folk in gun buses will speak my name in hushed tones of awe and wonder ... but I shall not boast about it (unlike many of the other chumps I shoot with), because I am *humble*.

But more often than I'd like, I'm barely mediocre, hitting the target between one in three or four shots. Then there are the days I genuinely wonder if someone isn't playing some sort of joke on me by removing all the lead from my cartridges. Either that or I've got a brain tumour because I'm doing the same thing I've been doing for years and nothing I point at is being dead. In fact, on those dark days, I'm honestly baffled where the shot is going – as if I'm pulling off some trick of cleverly shooting *between* birds. If it goes on too long, it starts to feel like flocks of partridge and pheasant are picking me to fly over as the safe option.

Oddly enough, those days aren't the worst. I've shot long enough to know that it's a wheel and it will come around and I will be back to my slightly averagey-normal soon enough. No, the worst days are those where you are behind by about the width of a hand, or offline by the same: the days where birds fly over and you injure them, so they flap by raggedly overhead, to land several hundred yards away where they may or may not be picked by someone's dog, or their leg drops or their tailfeathers explode and they don't quite drop. It probably would be best to stop shooting at this juncture, but we never do, to our shame. Instead, we keep pulling the trigger and hope it will get better than clean misses and 'pricked' birds.

On the subject of injured birds, increasingly a lot of people will go out of their way to avoid wringing something's neck with their bare hands. To this end, they'll often buy contraptions to distance themselves from the process – grisly pliers or 'priests' that they cosh the miserable poulet with so it dies of blood loss, *plus* a migraine. I find breaking a bird's neck the quickest and therefore most humane way and I'm quite prepared to do it mid drive to reduce the time something has to suffer.

There is another way of avoiding injuring birds, or, at least, reducing this greatly and that's shooting with a tighter choke or a smaller bore: your kill rate will go down as well, because you have to be more accurate but hey ho, I reckon two or three birds a drive is enough for anyone.

When all is said and done, formal, driven shooting is the best antidote to winter, with its boot stamping frosty build up, the sudden flushes and adrenaline rushes, its camaraderie, and a day spent outdoors when everyone else is huddled inside in front of a screen. As are the activities around it: the formalities and the log fires and pints when it's all over, with the dog wrapped around your chair leg at the bar– especially in the depths of Somerset, where I'm back today.

And, as I stand here, the drive just about to erupt, I remember how, in my last summer term, the abbey finally began to look attractive. In sunlight, not streaked with rain, the stonework looked closer to Cotswold honeyed than hewn granite, and the countryside softened as the fields and hedgerows filled out with fresh growth and wildflower. Between November and March, Somerset mud gets into everywhere and onto everything. Come May, footpaths, which had resembled routes through Ypres, were now pleasant places to walk with a book and some study notes to find a hollow of flattened grass in which to lie down awhile and fail miserably to revise.

As a result, Downside ended on a high: the exams were over and my career was mapped out in my seventeen-year-old head: university, army and comfortable retirement to write decept-ively comic poems in front of a fire.

Signing up to that public school thing of not taking anything too seriously helped me endure. The ever-present monastery; the black-clad monks striding across the quadrangles like cormorants of stern purpose; the refectory with its smells of stewing and broiling; the dank locker rooms; the stony, frigid showers that would transform thrice a day into a hammam of noise and pink bodies looming in the steam; and the sense that nothing really existed outside the walls except the village, a few fields, then ... space.

It defined me in those days, I think, just as a bevy of pheasants noisily break cover. A hen appears to my left, heading raggedly upwards and I shoulder the gun, part of my brain still in the past, wondering what my thirteen-year-old self would make of me ditching my poaching roots, my Dunlop wellies and hand-me-down anoraks for all this respectability.

Not much, I suspect. But, then again, what did I know?

December
GOOSE REVISITED

It's 5am, pitch dark and rainy, and I'm lying in a coffin. I'm trying to stop my teeth from chattering like those wind-up plastic ones you used to be able to buy in joke shops.

It's geese again, folks. Full circle.

I've swapped the genteel countryside of Oxfordshire for a wind-scrubbed peninsula on the Island of Orkney – though fuck knows why.

We're quite close to a village called Twat and I'm wondering if the joke is on us.

I suspect we could have come somewhere much closer to home to get rained on at a time I'm usually swaddled in a duvet – there seems to be geese everywhere, these days. The journey involved fighting our way around the M25, then fighting our way through weekend Heathrow crowds, ditto Edinburgh airport and onto a small but punchy-looking twin prop with 1970s seating that took us to the Island. Our hostess, the extremely lovely Kirsty, displayed the balance of a trapeze artist as she doled out shortbread and tea whilst we bumped along the lower atmosphere.

Things didn't get off to a good start: first of all, our hostess proved to be straight out of the *Great Expectations* playbook from tee off.

'I don't like shooting.' It was said in a way and followed up by a look that didn't so much mean that she disapproved of field sports in general, but rather the ones currently cluttering up her entrance hall. Our very own Miss Havisham was an unhappy woman from somewhere near Brighton. A husband hovered in

68

the background, vaguely apologetic but mainly just vague. But not as indistinct as the small boy we glimpsed over the course of the next few days – presumably their son but he might as well have been the apparition of someone who lived there in another century – when the house was a house, not a sombre hotel with chilly rooms, large expanses of carpet through lack of furniture and noisy taps that belched brownish water. The boy would sometimes appear in an open door, then retreat on your approach like a meek spectre.

There was a book nook with a dubious mix of middle-aged soft porn by Jackie Collins and Jilly Cooper and 1970s bedtime stories. There was also a study-cum-sewing room – neither activity something I'd equate with a holiday on Orkney. Although it does rain a lot.

We met the bloke who was organising the shooting when we went to our restaurant later. As we were tucking into roasted goose breasts plus gallons of Malbec to wash it all down, he loped in and sat at our table with a big grin on his face.

'Welcome to Orkney!' he said as if he'd invented the whole series of islands all by himself. 'How was the trip up?'

We assured him it was super and that we'd been having a lovely time from the moment we'd kissed our wives goodbye and got in the car ... and added (sincerely) that the food was excellent – we were looking forward to getting some of our own geese for turning into delicious roast dinners.

'So, you've all got guns?' he asked.

'Um, no,' we replied. 'We thought you were providing them.' There was a brief but significant silence.

'Yes, yes of course,' our host said, a look of very poorly disguised panic crossing his face, ' ... I've just got to, um ... I'll be back shortly.'

In the end it worked out: four guns arrived at our hotel just before we went to bed. Three were semi-auto, single barrelled affairs encased in camouflaged plastic – ideal for wildfowling. The fourth was where our chap's panicky whip round had come up short: a side-by-side that had seen better days – stubby and loose-hinged. It also turned out to be 'my' gun by popular consent. Alone in my room, I inspected it: no maker's mark, it had never been remotely a good gun and I seriously doubted whether I should be putting 40 gram goose shot down it.

So, this consideration was also on my mind the next morning about an hour before dawn, along with whether I was going to succumb to hypothermia or drowning first.

Drowning might be an odd concern to have when you're in the middle of a field, on top of a hill, but that's because one is rarely lying flat on one's back in a container, listening to the rain wondering if it will eventually fill up with you in it.

I think I ought to explain a bit about the coffin at this juncture. Geese tend to spend their days on dry land and their nights on water. Not exclusively, but as a rule, which explains why the footpaths along the Thames are mainly made of goose poo – until it rains and then they turn into goose slurry. Creeping up on them before dawn whilst they bob about on dark inland bays dreaming goosey dreams of pristine walkways and jetties they can make into death traps by taking hundreds of slimy dumps on them is easy enough and you'll get quite close. However, the minute it gets light and they take to the air to find something nice to eat, they'll spot you and go somewhere else. Hides are the traditional solution but a 'coffin' has definite benefits, in that it is very portable and easy to install in the dark. You just need to cover it with bits of the countryside (grass, straw, sticks) and you've got your own mini-hide with an easy-opening door.

Probably the most entertaining part of the process is the expression on the goose's face when the ghillie shouts "Goose" and you burst out of your tomb, like a gun-toting vampire, and shoot it.

The other benefit over a hide is once you've set up your coffin and camouflaged it, you can catch up on some of your lost sleep by taking a snooze in the warm confines of your temporary grave.

Jumping out on very surprised geese turns out to be a brilliant way to spend a morning and more than makes up for the early start and terrible weather.

Even when the competition arrives in the form of a seagull as it did on our first morning.

One of the geese is limply flapping a few yards from us. It's probably dead, or very nearly and, as there seems to be an interdiction on jumping out of your 'coffin' and gathering up fallen birds, we stay put and watch as the new arrival as it plumps down beside the fallen goose. The gull has that customary deranged look in its beady eyes.

'Arghh! I've been shot,' you can imagine the goose whimpering.

The seagull looks down at the dying bird, then up at us watching it.

Then it pecks the goose in the face.

'Oi!' we shout, 'go away, you horrible seagull, that's our nearly dead goose and that's a not a nice thing to do.'

The seagull responds with a defiant look and jabs its large yellow beak, like a giant incisor, into the goose's stomach – more or less, I imagine, where it's been shot.

I'm seriously thinking about blowing the seagull's head off at this juncture but something about not liking to shoot anything I'm not prepared to eat stops me. One of the other guns eventually fires a warning shot a few yards from its webbed feet. The seagull hops off and then almost immediately hops back to take its station next to the goose. Before we up the ante, the situation is resolved by the goose dying and the seagull losing interest in something helpless it can no longer torment during its final moments. It flaps off, presumably to find an orphan child's ice cream it can steal. If seagull shooting became a thing, I'd be first in the queue.

We're done by 9am but we're still late for breakfast in the House of Ill Will. This leads to a lot of huffing and puffing from our landlady about breakfast being ruined and a lot of profuse *thank yous* from us when plates of slightly congealed sausages etc are banged on the table. The husband is even less in evidence although the boy makes a brief appearance to be shoo'ed back behind the door leading to their private quarters, like a consumptive. The place used to belong to the Bell family, of whisky fame. I bet it was happier then.

After a trip to look at the prehistoric village of Skara Brae, tea and a nice afternoon nap we're ready for round two.

Shoreline shooting is a revelation: it's like rock pooling but with a gun. We park the Land Rover on a hill above by a small stone cottage and take a path leading through some fields to the beach, the ghillie and his labrador leading the way. The general idea is to catch wildfowl as they fly back from the fields to rest up on the calmer patches of sea or on the lakes and ponds scattered about behind the sandbanks and reeds. Typically, I imagine it was mainly duck but geese are staying in greater numbers in Scotland all year round and breeding, presumably. This means they're literally everywhere.

Shoreline shooting can therefore be mainly geese, with a smattering of duck and even the odd pheasant with an identity crisis. Some types of duck are off limits, ditto geese, which turned out to be tricky as dusk starts to settle.

We are posted at various points where it's safe and I find my-self standing on a collection of flat rocks, alone with the docile swell of the sea a few feet away, the fast-diminishing light, and my thoughts. Soon there is just a pale strip of blue edged grey on the horizon and I find it hard to locate a seaweed-free spot along the shoreline I am trying to patrol. So, I opt to stay put. The early shots we had, the visibility was good but I'm now firing at winged shadows that appear out of the gloom, like raptors. This is a strangely ethereal, almost dreamlike version of hunting, quite unlike anything I've ever done before. I take a shot at a duck and miss, but someone gets it further down the line.

Then it goes quiet and, bit by bit, my mind starts to drift again. I am beginning to think that's it for the evening, when a greylag comes over me like a silent bomber, a familiar outline against a dark sky. It's almost night now, so I know this is my last shot of our short holiday. As ever, it's all the truer for being instinctive – genetic rules favouring humans who can bring down a moving target, which you wonder if we might lose, now we've got Asda. In the end, by luck more than judgement, it's about as perfect a shot as you can hope for as the bird's neck snaps back as the majority of the gun's pattern hits it in the head. It splashes down and, yet again, the useless human being is saved by a dog. Our labrador, of the bull-necked and barrel-chested variety, has tracked its trajectory and is already swimming out to get it.

As we walk silently back to the car, our head torches throwing flickering beams out across the hawthorn, grass and gorse, I'm already looking forward to a pint, then dinner. For now, though, I'm happy to tramp back in silence – the weight of my gun in one hand, precious goose in the other.

Much of life is about balance.

Epilogue

When I tell people that I very much like the countryside, they nod, and you can see vaguely appreciative thoughts going on behind their eyes.

Not always (but nearly always), when I expand on the theme and start to talk about using the great outdoors as a larder and not just a place to potter about in, their eyes narrow.

'You mean shooting?'

'Um, well, yes,' I admit, already wishing I hadn't brought it up, ' ... and a bit of fishing, foraging ... and the dog gets a good walk, learns a few skills, um ... '

'So, you enjoy killing things?'

And I know I'm on very thin social ice, because who – in their right mind – would admit to that? Then again, it's exactly what I've just said I like doing.

On one level, the question-come-accusation is a little unjust – or, at least, it's more complicated than that. For starters, I also very much like picking berries and mushrooms, which is blameless – unless it involves stealing from other people's gardens, which, to be fair, has been known. Fundamentally, I like the idea of any food that hasn't gone through a chemical process and a complicated supply chain before it gets to you. But, leaving aside the uncontroversial foraging, it's not as if I routinely hoick fish out of the water and chuck them into the nearest hedge. Or track a pigeon falling out of the sky, as I blow the smoke off my barrels, smirk, then saunter home ... via KFC.

I believe that if you do hunt, you should eat what you kill, or what's the point. For one thing, I'm pretty sure it's better for you than shop-bought: containing less additives or genetic time bombs. It's cheaper and it's nearly always far tastier because it has been allowed to live a bit how nature intended. Until you murdered it ... hmm.

So very far from innocent but, that said, I think those of us who choose to eat meat or fish are far too removed from the process. In my more militant mood swings, I suggest to anyone in earshot that all 'food' should still be alive when you buy it in a shop and that it's up to you to take it home, usher it through the door, then kill it before the kids get back from school. Or even get them to help because, if you're not prepared to get blood on your hands, then perhaps it would be more honest to be a vegetarian.

Then again, taking a cleaver to a chicken's neck in cold blood in the utility room, whilst you swig wine would not be the nice, relaxing lead up to supper, in the same way that chopping carrots is.

And *hunting* adds another layer – and this is where my complainant has a point re the whole 'enjoyment of killing issue'.

Getting the better of quarry, through some skill and by dint of forward-facing eyes and opposable thumbs, whilst not 'fun' in the strictest sense of the word, is undeniably exciting. We're hard-wired hunter gatherers. As a shooting friend of mine once put it, when you have taught the dog well, and the birds take to the air in roughly the right direction, or you have spent hours creeping up on something that is faster, with several hundred times better hearing than you ... and the exact moment you squeeze the trigger and whatever you are aiming at drops, then as a man you know right then and there just what you were put on Planet Earth to do.

Right or wrong, there is no getting away from the fact that two million years of conditioning has turned a vital necessity to put food on the table into a sport, which you also have to admit is a pretty blokey thing to do.

But you can't really say all that to someone you've just met at a party, because it can get a bit ranty, so I usually keep quiet and hope they don't spit in my wine when I've gone to the loo.

Re-reading what I have written, it strikes me that the best memories I have in the field (or a field) are wrapped up in friends and family. I greatly enjoy rough shooting, just the dog and me, but it's not the same. There's no-one to laugh at you when you fuck up, for starters, or mock your dress sense and disparage your abilities – in short, do all those things British men only feel comfortable doing with their best friends.

I've enjoyed writing this book if only because it's always pleasant to recall episodes of your life with largely happy outcomes – hindsight is the bitter-sweet end of the learning curve and makes up a large part of you who you turn into.

It's also reminded me that much of life has something to do with death, like it or not: whether that is taking a risk and living to tell the tale, personal loss or putting food on the table. Friendship and field sports do the same job here, which is why they go so well together: they soften the harsher realities. And this is a good lesson for life, because when the world seems to be precarious and cruel, remember that the game is never up, there's everything to play for.

And, mostly, it will all be OK.

To every man upon this earth
Death cometh soon or late.
And how can man die better
Than facing fearful odds,
For the ashes of his fathers,
And the temples of his Gods ...

'Horatius'
by Thomas Babington Macaulay

Writing is a team effort and, as ever, I am indebted to a host of people who helped make this book a lot less bad. So heartfelt gratitude goes to Alex Cotter for her sound and sane editorial advice, the same for Nick G as well as his skill and patience designing books and making sense of my grammar. To Keith Jennings for sanity checking my scant knowledge of the technical and factual side of shooting and finally to Jude Francis Bennett for having to put up with me as a father and for his brilliant illustrations that are easily the best bit of the book.

When Robin grew up, he thought he wanted to be a soldier until everyone else realised that putting him in charge of a tank was a very bad idea. He then became an assistant gravedigger, a private tutor to the rich and famous, entrepreneur ... until finally settling down to write improbable stories to stop his children killing each other on long car journeys. He once heard himself described on the radio travel news as 'some twit' when his car broke down and blocked the rush hour traffic around Marble Arch. This is about right. Robin is married with three children, one of whom illustrated this book. He spends his time between France and England.

@writer_robin

Jude grew up in the south of France in the Pyrenees in a place his friends like to aptly call 'the middle of nowhere', although this only meant that he spent most of his time outside in nature with his brother.

He has now just left school and is working on a building site to afford travelling around south-east Asia and Australia with his girlfriend. Aside from being bossed around by an angry Middle-aged man on the weekdays at work, he enjoys playing rugby and drawing, which is why he's delighted to have scribbled down the illustrations for this book during his lunch breaks.

Printed in Great Britain
by Amazon

9dcfdaf4-d349-41a0-bcb0-0ee03715054dR01